Bully
IN THE
Mirror

Making Hate Stop When
You Don't Think You Can

SHANAYA FASTJE

CHANGING LIVES PRESS

The information contained in this book is based upon the research and personal experiences of the author. It is not intended as a substitute for consulting with your physician or another healthcare provider. Any attempt to diagnose and treat an illness should be done under the direction or a healthcare professional. The publisher and author are not responsible for the any adverse effects or consequences resulting from the use of or procedures discussed in this book. Should the reader have any questions, the author and publisher strongly suggest consulting a professional healthcare provider.

Changing Lives Press • www.changinglivespress.com

To purchase our books, please visit our website at
www.continentalsalesinc.com
or contact Terry Wybel, Continental Sales, Inc.,
at wybelt@wybel.com or call 1-847-381-6530.

Our titles are focused on books that impact lives. The authors
we choose are those who have influenced or changed the
way we think, act, or process ideas and information.

EDITOR: Michele Matrisciani
ILLUSTRATIONS: Shanaya Fastje
COVER and INTERIOR DESIGN: Gary A. Rosenberg

Printed in the United States of America

10   9   8   7   6   5   4   3   2   1

Contents

To all the children who are
survivors or victims of bullying.
You are the spirit that has inspired
me to advocate for your cause.
May the mirror that I pass on
to you provide you with the
strength that you need to get
you through the torment.

Introduction

I became aware that kids were committing suicide because of ongoing bullying. It sickened me so much that bullying was actually causing kids to take their own lives that I wanted to do what I could to become a part of a solution to an ongoing problem that I hear adults talking about all the time.

I knew about some kinds of bullying because of some of the things that happened to my friends and me. We are all victims of some form of bullying. *Whether you are being bullied, have been a witness to someone being bullied, are the parent or teacher of someone who is being bullied, or are a bully yourself, you are a victim.*

I know what you're thinking. *Did Shanaya just say that bullies were victims? How could she? They are evil and bad and are the ones victimizing. How can she say they are victims when so many kids are suffering to the point where they think killing themselves is a better thing to do than telling someone who might be able to help, or confronting the bully, or even fighting back?*

The first defense against bullies is to understand why a bully is a bully. They're victims in that they are insecure, scared, succumbing to peer pressure, or even acting out personal problems they are having at home. Many times if we understand who a bully really is, it freaks us out less. Being less scared of them helps keep us stronger against them.

Bullies are no different from you or me. In fact, if you look in the mirror and examine your thoughts about yourself, you probably would have a lot in common with what bullies worry about. Here's an exercise that you can try. Look in the mirror, empower yourself by thinking that the bully in your life could be staring right back at you. Imagine the bully—what does the bully look like? Tall or short, fat or thin? Practice facing the bully and envision yourself staring him or her down. Do they have bad teeth or good teeth? Are they wearing glasses or have braces? That's right, they are in fact no different from you or me, and that is what you need to keep telling yourself. After a while, you will find that the bully in the mirror isn't as scary or powerful as you thought, and boy is that a cool feeling! It's like when you were little and were scared of the monster hiding in the closet. Once you pulled the door open, you saw there was really nothing there at all.

I hope this book will not only help you see the truth about bullies, but it will give you the confidence and the strategies needed to help get you through bullying without feeling like there is no way out. You don't have to feel helpless. That's why I spent hours reading about bullying so that I could help. Yes, I was bullied and witnessed bullying while I was in school, but it never got that bad.

I wanted to learn as much about bullying as I could. Now with all my new knowledge I wanted to come up with an idea that could help me share it with as many kids as I could. I wanted to help other kids to understand what I had learned and to give them action steps to protect themselves from the viciousness of bullying. Then I had an idea. If we learn in school through curriculum taught by teachers, then what if there was a curriculum that educates about bullying? That's when I started to write one full speed ahead.

After weeks of writing, my twenty-eight-page study was ready to be tested. I became trigger happy and printed hundreds of my curriculum and stacked them on top of my desk. *Yikes!* I thought. *Now what am I gonna do?* Handing out the curriculum became my next goal. The trunk of my mom's car was filled with the copies of my anti-bullying curriculum, and the next thing you know, we became a delivery service, passing out the curriculum throughout our city of El Paso, Texas, one neighborhood at a time.

It was a tiring job, which seemed like full time, and after I handed out the last of the curricula, I began speaking at schools to help kids learn the "Bully in the Mirror" concept, and how to protect themselves and give them a safe place to feel free to talk about bullying. Speaking to so many different kids all over El Paso allowed me to choose from the audience and build what I call "anti-bullying teams." It gets the attention of the audience each time we do it.

I felt like I really wasn't doing enough. This needed to be bigger than what I was already doing. If I was going to help make a major difference, I had to reach more kids and find new ways to educate them about where bullying comes from, why it happens, who it happens to, and once again, let everyone realize that we are all in some form or another victims of bullying, even the bullies themselves.

Bully in the Mirror is for kids and about kids by a kid. It is based on other kids and their experiences of being bullied and bullying. I think parents can read it too. My parents did. In fact, getting adults more involved is one of the tips you'll read about in this book. Some people who read this book might say, "She's just a kid." Well, I am more than just a kid. I am a kid who cares. And I'm no different from a lot of kids out there who have compassion and talent and lots to give, if only their positive energy could be freed up.

My hope for this book is to send the message that kids can create positive change in the face of the horrible epidemic of bullying. We all have a unique part in this change, and I hope in this book, you will find yours.

❖ One out of four kids is bullied.

❖ One in seven students in grades K through 12 is either a bully or a victim of bullying.

❖ 100,000 students carry a weapon to school and have witnessed violence at home.

❖ National Education Association surveys show that 282,000 students are physically attacked in secondary schools each month and 90 percent of fourth through eighth graders report being victims of bullying.

❖ American Federation of Teachers surveys of bullying episodes in which peers intervened, 57 percent of the interventions were effective. Peers intervene in only 11 to 19 percent of all bullying incidents.

❖ According to the Bureau of Justice, teenagers say revenge is the strongest motivation for school shootings. Add on top of that, kids who are obese, gay, or have disabilities are 63 percent more likely to be bullied than other children.

The most interesting thing I learned, which I found very helpful when figuring out workable strategies to overcome bullying is: boys and girls get bullied in very different ways and react differently too.

Bully in the Mirror is your get-real guide that gives you tools that work and information that will make you unafraid of bullies and prevent you and others from being bullied in the future. It takes the power away from bullies and puts it in your hands to do whatever you want to in life, and that includes protecting yourself in the future from being or becoming bullies.

In this book, you'll learn:

- Why bullies act so mean.
- The signs that someone is being bullied.
- Why bullying is so harmful.
- Key ways to stop bullies in their tracks.
- How to build strong anti-bullying teams at your school.
- How teachers and parents can help.

A good shortcut to remember as you read this book is a bully's power is fake, just like the monsters in your closet. They only have power if you give your own power to them! If you can move on and learn to sleep with the closet door open, then nothing can stop you from staring down that bully in the mirror, once and for all. The bullies don't stand a chance!

1

Bullying Basics

I feel tha, if you are somehow influenced to write something horrible, untrue, and hurtful about someone, you should sign your name as the sender. But the likelihood of this happening is very slight. Why? Because by signing you are telling the world who you are—a person who wants to hurt others, regardless of whether or not what you are writing is true. That's why you should think before you speak if it causes the same effect as if you were writing a signed letter. Remember your words of hate will come back to haunt you.

I do believe that some kids are hateful enough to

take the gamble of signing their names. That's why bullying on social networks happens; everyone can see who is saying nasty things, and the chances of your coming out a winner are very slim.

If you're looking for instant attention and will do just about anything to get it, why not stand on your head instead? At the very least it would be an entertaining to others. Negative attention, while attention, is still . . . negative. If you want attention, there are tons of ways to go about getting the positive kind.

Don't do things simply because you desire attention and then have a ton of bricks drop on your head. Think before you do something, and if your gut instinct tells you and screams at you, "This is stupid!" then it *is* stupid. Stupidity creates more stupidity. If this is your game, don't fall victim to playing it. Simply walk away. I'll guarantee a protective barrier from "stupid" getting to you.

Typically, I hate the word "stupid"; it's a pet peeve of mine. But the reality is some kids feel the need to try something stupid. Choose the other "S" word instead—"smart."

Smart makes me feel good.

Smart makes me do good.

Smart keeps me scared when I need to be and gets me out of being scared when I can't afford to be.

Smart keeps my spirit in me.

Smart is much more deserving, and smart knows that the best part of life is to love, even in your darkest fight against bullying.

Smart is in everybody.

Smart makes healthy decisions for a better you.

Speak Up. When you talk loudly and strongly enough for the bully to hear, you have taken away their false power.

As you go through this book, come back to this chapter. On the lines below, write down important words and what they mean to you. Make your own personal diary to help you remember how to stand up against bullies!

_____

_____

_____

_____

_____

_____

_____

Here's another exercise to try. Answer the questions below:

❖ Who have you seen being bullied?

❖ What was happening at the time?

❖ Why do you think it was happening then?

❖ What do you think the bully was thinking?

❖ What do you think the victim was thinking?

❖ Did the bystander(s) do anything?

❖ What do you think they were thinking?

❖ Unless you were the bully, did anyone do anything about it?

❖ What do you think should have been done?

BULLY BREAKDOWN

Before we get started learning how to protect ourselves from bullying, preventing it, or helping turn around the attitudes of the bullies that are out there, we need to understand the basics of bullying. Who is the bully? What are the types of bullying, and how does bullying affect boys and girls differently? Since bullies look for people who are physically weaker than they are, are more insecure, and have been rejected because they don't have many social skills, it could be safely said that those are the exact things bullies see in themselves. Bullies pick on people to prove that they have power.

They want to look good, but the whole time they're hoping no one will confront them. That's because all bullies are cowards. A big mistake bystanders make is to laugh at the victim or cheer on the bully. Bullies need that. It's the only way they can feel confident enough to do it again. So, let's meet this so-called bully.

"Bullies are cowards."

WHO IS A BULLY?

Anyone can become a bully. Girls aren't looked at anymore as being all pink and glittery, bursting with niceness. Mean girls are a growing problem today, and if moms and dads step in and teach their daughters how to treat others nicely, there would be fewer mean girls.

Boys might not always be tall and handsome and respectful. Some fathers may not be teaching their sons how to be nice. Instead, they focus on toughness, sports, and mild forms of violence, like they see in the movies or in video games. Not all guys are going to be football players! Dads and moms should teach their sons that being kind doesn't make them weak. It's actually a sign of strength.

Girls tend to inflict pain by playing with your head. Their games are sometimes referred to as "head games." Have you ever heard of that term? Head games can make you feel like you're going crazy half the time. You feel like maybe one day a girl likes you and the next she is cold. Or her head games can be so strong that sometimes you think you imagined something she did or actually begin to believe you are the one to blame.

Girls use words to bully more than they use physical forms of bullying. Girl bullies thrive on gossip, rumors, and put-downs. When boys bully, they tend to use physical force; maybe they will shove or pull you by the hood, rather than challenge you with words.

Even if you didn't intend to be mean, sometimes we all lose our tempers. If this happens to you, remember that it's okay to make a mistake now and then. Just be aware of what you've done and try not to make the same mistake again.

TYPES OF BULLYING

The most common types of bullying are:

- **Verbal.** This is an emotional form of bullying that includes name-calling, teasing, insults, and gossip. It's like the girl stuff I just talked about before.

- **Physical.** This kind of bullying uses physical force. It includes pushing, bumping, hitting, and stealing or destroying the victim's belongings. While this is mostly a boy thing, more and more girls are hitting, pulling hair, and finding ways to use physical force. I've even seen grown women on television try to beat each other up or push each other.

- **Cyberbullying.** This is the sneakiest form of bullying. It spreads verbal bullying through email, social networking websites, blogs, texts, and tweets.

- **Hazing.** This is forcing someone to do something before they are allowed to be part of a group. This used to be something you only heard about with kids in college, but now it has come to a school near you!

Different kinds of bullying show up in different places. Most physical bullying happens off school grounds like at the bus stop and in kids' neighborhoods. Bullies wait until they are away from adults before getting violent.

Verbal abuse hurts in a much different way. You don't get scared about being hurt physically, but you get scared inside. Words are used as weapons. All weapons do damage. Dealing with it means knowing that you don't have to do it alone. Get help!

It's pretty frightening to know that bullying might go beyond pushing into punching or kicking. But the pain that words cause can be just as awful. How someone is being bullied doesn't matter. What is important is to get it to *stop,* and *fast.*

MISGUIDED LOVE

Misguided love is something exhibited by a so-called friend or even a family member. The usual scenario goes something like this: you get invited somewhere, maybe to the movies or the mall, and you're having a really good time. You're happy to get out of the house and have some fun. But you end up at a store somehow and this person you're with dares you, "Come on, don't be a chicken and just take the key chain; they won't even notice it's gone." In the process, she says that if you don't take it, you won't be cool anymore. So, at that moment you have to make a decision: listen to that person or listen to your gut.

This scenario in which you are lured into a situation that makes you feel uncomfortable under the label of friendship is what I call "misguided love," because your "friend" is misguiding you, making you believe that he or she cares for you and wants to spend time with you. This is a form of hazing, which was just mentioned earlier. So if you choose to listen and take that key chain, how do you think it will make you feel afterward? Is it something you could go home and willingly share excitedly with your parents, or is it going to be something you hide from them to avoid punishment and/or shame?

Just think about it: somebody just tried to convince you to do something very wrong, so why would you even consider it? There are many other ways to do exciting things that are right. Look, we are all destined to make mistakes, but the ones we learn from are the things that we do by our own choice, not because we are hazed into doing them. Sometimes kids come up with a million excuses to do something like, "I want (so and so) to still be my friend, so I'll do whatever she wants me to do," or "I just don't care if I get caught or not."

Whatever the case may be, hazing is indeed a form

of bullying and it takes your power away. Doing something out of peer pressure doesn't make you a better person and it doesn't get you more friends. Staying focused on the good things, and knowing how and when to say no, is keeping true to who you are.

EXCUSES, EXCUSES

When parents, teachers, or even kids make excuses for bullying, it's almost like sending a message that says, "It's not serious enough for us to worry about it." And if that message is spreading, how do you think bullying will end? It won't. Here are some things people shouldn't say about bullying, because these are the statements that keep us from making progress in the fight against bullying:

SHOULDN'T SAY: "Bullying is normal; we all go through it."

SHOULD SAY: "Bullying is not normal, and you don't have to go through it alone."

SHOULDN'T SAY: "I've already spoken to the school about my child being bullied. Let's see what happens."

SHOULD SAY: "I'll revisit with the school as many times as it takes to help my child."

SHOULDN'T SAY: "Boys should toughen up and not be so wimpy."

SHOULD SAY: "It doesn't matter if you're a boy, bullying is not acceptable. Boys have feelings too and should be free to express them just as girls do. Holding back how you feel doesn't make you a man."

SHOULDN'T SAY: "I think there is something wrong with my child, but I'm not sure what could be bothering him."

SHOULD SAY: "I will make it my priority to get to the bottom of what is bothering my child and help him."

SHOULDN'T SAY: "Girls just gossip. It's harmless; that's what girls do."

SHOULD SAY: "Girls are using their mouths as weapons, and there is no excuse for it."

SHOULDN'T SAY: "I'm so tired of my child getting bullied over and over again."

SHOULD SAY: "The first time it happened is one too many. I will not allow my child to continue getting bullied."

SHOULDN'T SAY: "There is nothing I can do about bullying. The schools can do whatever they want."

SHOULD SAY: "Schools care about my child. Together we can find a solution."

SHOULDN'T SAY: "I'm scared to go to school because of bullying."

SHOULD SAY: "I am scared to go to school because of bullying, but I will not let them win."

SHOULDN'T SAY: "My friends make me bully other kids because if I don't, they won't be my friends anymore."

SHOULD SAY: "Nobody can make me do something that I don't want to do, and real friends don't haze."

SHOULDN'T SAY: "I can't tell my parents I'm being bullied because I will get in trouble."

SHOULD SAY: "I will tell my parents I am being bullied. They need to know."

SHOULDN'T SAY: "I always see bullying happen, but I don't want to get involved."

SHOULD SAY: "The bystander is the key to reduce bullying. We all must get involved."

SHOULDN'T SAY: "I wish bullying didn't exist."

SHOULD SAY: "I know bullying exists, but I will be part of the solution."

SHOULDN'T SAY: "My dad bullies me, and I'm scared of him."

SHOULD SAY: "My dad bullies me and I'm scared of him, but I will talk to someone about it."

SHOULDN'T SAY: "I hate school because of bullying."

SHOULD SAY: "I hate school because of bullying, but it won't take me down."

SHOULDN'T SAY: "I am failing in school because I can't concentrate. I worry too much about bullying."

SHOULD SAY: "I will do whatever it takes in school to learn."

SHOULDN'T SAY: "If you tell someone you are being bullied it's going to get worse."

SHOULD SAY: "You must tell someone you are being bullied; you're not alone."

SHOULDN'T SAY: "As long as they don't hit you, it's not bullying."

SHOULD SAY: "There are many forms of bullying, and it all hurts."

If you have gotten to a point in your life that is so low that you feel you don't care about yourself enough, than you have got to find a sense of redirection to re-evaluate your goals, morals, and future. Just because you're a kid does not mean you cannot start thinking about your future. You actually need to start thinking about your future as a kid. It's better to be home feeling bored out of your mind than to be out listening to your so-called friends persuade you into doing bad things that inside you don't want to do. Being bored is just another excuse, and boredom has a solution, just like anything else; you can always think of something to do.

The temptations that your so-called friends put upon you, are what I call, "bullies in disguise." They pretend they are your friends, but real and true friends don't haze or try to get you in trouble. A real friend will tell you just the opposite: "Don't do it. It's not worth it." So if you're feeling bored at home, use your imagination. There is a quote by Albert Einstein that I just absolutely love and believe: "Imagination is more important than knowledge."

WORDS TO LEARN

Before you read the rest of this book, I want to give you a few very important words. Understanding how I use them will help you address even the worst bully in your school.

Bully. A person who is mean to others, mostly those who they think are weaker than them. A bully is all about using fake power. The power seems real to the victim. Bullies know that if they can take away your power, it will be hard for you to get that power back.

Victim. This is the person who is being bullied. If you are a victim, you are cheating yourself by thinking that you don't have power to make it stop. Reach out to others for help. Even if you don't succeed the first time, the second time you'll be stronger, and maybe you'll learn to confront your bully or just plain ignore her. Keep trying. You deserve it!

Bystander. Anyone who sees someone being bullied. Some of them are even adults. Some bystanders say and do nothing to help the victim or to stop the bully. Others choose to let the victim know they aren't alone. If you are a bystander, it's important not to put yourself in danger. Later you will learn lots of ways to take action safely.

Courage. When you face danger, you have courage. When kids worry about a bully, they forget about the "C" word. To deal with bullying you must show courage. That's easier said than done! I happen to have a little bit of natural courage but that wouldn't be enough to stand right in front of a bully who is a large force of human ugliness! When I say ugliness, I mean what's on the inside, not how the bully looks. And that's frightening.

We aren't born with courage, but everyone can learn how to develop it. I think of it as a skill that needs lots and lots of attention. Develop courage by changing small things one at a time, each and every day. For example, if in your daily routine, you are someone who says to yourself, "I just can't do it. . . ." it could mean passing a test, speaking up for yourself, running a mile, etc. You're on the attack, except the victim is you.

> *"Develop courage by changing small things one at a time, each and every day."*

When you attack yourself, you become your worst enemy. But as powerful as you believe your negative thoughts are, they can be changed into positive, self-trusting, and loving thoughts so you can respect and love yourself.

Start by checking in on a daily basis and having an inner dialogue with yourself. If your negative dialogue says "You can't do it," instead say, "I am capable of doing it," But being vague with the word "it" is not as powerful as reciting your specific goals. Don't know what they are or how to get started? Ask someone to help you with a particular subject you're struggling with. Say to any-one—a friend, teacher, parent, or sibling—"I'm in need of your help." Don't think about the fear of rejection in reaching out. That fear is only based in the temporary space of the unknown. Getting out of your comfort zone is a tough task, but once you find someone to accompany you on your journey outside that zone, your courage will develop until you feel independent and confident enough in other goals.

And remember, you are not alone in these miserable self-doubts. Everyone goes through them, and everyone has the ability to change them. Courage means to train yourself by taking action. It is not enough to just think about building courage; it won't happen if you just think about it. By taking action, your energy moves you from being stuck. Every small step is what takes you there, because trying to do it all at once will be much more difficult. Smaller and daily steps are better than one big, huge step. The practice of building courage is crucial. If you don't repeat it on a daily basis, it'll vanish. Use it or lose it!

The most courageous thing you can do, by the way,

is taking responsibility or "ownership" for the challenges before you. You can't change the fact that these good or bad things are happening, but you can change the way your react to them. It is your choice how you let it affect you. If you're being bullied, there are so many choices you have in reacting. You could choose to not stand up for yourself, you can stoop to the bully's level, you could allow his or her mean actions to define who you think you are, you could give up, or you could turn into a bully yourself, and on and on. . . . Instead of blaming others, "own" what has happened. Every day, make the decision to be willing to do what is right in order to receive the good and the bad. Don't feel you have the answer to everything but rather the questions to ask. Yes, it takes courage to ask questions, but the more you do it every day, the easier it will get.

A Dream for a Day

On the morning of each new day, create a dream for the day, because dreaming gets you closer to the dream. For example, wake up and tell yourself, "Today my dream will be to share a fear with someone." By sharing fears with people you trust, you might find that your fear may be the same as someone else's, and you will learn that everyone has fears. This will help build on your fears one at a time, instead of letting all of the fears get bigger and bigger, until they paralyze you.

You can tell yourself that you have the right to voice any concerns as much as anyone else does. The more you speak up every day, it becomes a habit. In other words, if nothing changes, nothing happens. Change "nothings" to "somethings." That is what builds great leaders. Think every single day what are your needs, wants, and fears and work on them. If you do this, the pain you feel when the bully is bothering you will slowly disappear.

Respect

Respect means that you don't judge people or hold things against others just for being different. We are all different from one another. Respect means you can feel good about others and their special qualities or way of life, even if they are not yours. Instead of being afraid of kids who are different, respect their differences. Other people have the right to view things their own way . . . just like you have the right to view things your own way! This reminds me of another word, "tolerance," which means you live in a world with people, who, even if they look or act differently, believe differently, or live differently, live peacefully among each other.

Don't neglect respect! I couldn't do all the things I do if I didn't respect the people I'm trying to help. Even if they don't like what I say, I still respect them. My message comes straight from my heart.

BULLYING: A QUICK REVIEW

Verbal Bullying

- Making a victim feel like they caused the problem
- Name-calling
- Insults
- Making fun of physical appearance
- Threatening to cause physical harm
- Telling someone to kill themselves

Verbal Social Bullying

- Gossiping
- Negative comments
- Teasing
- Targeting race, religion, gender, intelligence, abilities, or sexual preference
- Cyberbulling
- Making fun of family and friends of victim

Cyberbullying

- Anonymous threatening emails
- A fake profile on a social-networking site using a student's real name, photo, and so on
- Spammed with name-calling posts that spread rumors about a specific student
- Name-calling in chat rooms

Physical Bullying

- Threatening gestures, like the middle finger, giving dirty looks, or raising fists
- Damaging property or schoolwork
- Pushing/shoving or kicking/tripping
- Stealing personal property or schoolwork

Physical Social Bullying

- Excluding someone from a group
- Ignoring someone
- Hazing

REALITY CHECK

Bullying happens at many different levels. It doesn't have to be an all-out fistfight. Because it can creep up on you, the following is a short list of questions to see if you've ever accidentally bullied someone else. Be honest with your answers. No one will see this except you.

1. Telling someone that you can't be friends is wrong. Have you ever told anyone this?

2. Have you ever felt bad about something you said to someone?

3. Has your anger ever taken over?

4. Have you ever pushed, shoved, or bumped against someone?

5. Have you ever threatened someone because you were angry with a different person like a friend or relative?

6. Are you hot-tempered? Even with adults?

7. Do the people you hang out with engage in bad behavior?

8. Do you feel bad for kids who are bullied?

9. Have you ever been bullied by another kid or a parent?

10. Do you encourage your friends to act inappropriately?

11. Do you threaten others to get what you need?

Maybe your answers to these questions surprised you, and you realized you have been partaking in some bullying behavior yourself without really meaning to. I don't mean for this quiz to make you feel bad about yourself or anybody you might know who has done any of these things. The point is to show how even the smallest actions can be harmful to others' self-esteem and well-being. Being aware of our actions—the good ones and the bad ones—makes us accountable to ourselves and to everybody else.

Can you imagine how much easier we could get along at school, in communities, on playgrounds, and so on, if we all took ownership of our actions? Gone would be a world in which we dismissed each other as fellow human beings. With this new mutual respect for ourselves and each other, bullying would be buried deep beneath the earth's surface.

2

Being Bullied

Bullying creates a lot of bad feelings like fear and sadness. More kids today than ever say they are depressed, nervous, and lonely. Some are even taking medication to help them deal with these emotions. That's because some kids take words more seriously than others. They start to believe all the hurtful, hateful things being said about them.

The longer bullying goes on, the more hopeless victims feel. It doesn't take long before they're trapped in their own minds. Sadness takes over everything. They can't enjoy the sports or games or movies that used to make them happy. Without any kind of relief, they think there is no way out.

UNFRIENDING IN REAL LIFE

Since elementary school, three very close friends did just about everything together. A few years later the girls were in junior high. One day Molly caught up with Hazel and Amber in the hallway. Molly noticed that Amber was acting strange but had no idea why. As they walked down the hall together, Molly asked Hazel why Amber was acting weird. Hazel acted like she hadn't heard the question.

The bell rang so Molly didn't have time to ask again. All during class, Amber passed notes to other girls. After reading the notes, all of them would turn to look at Molly. Then they would all giggle.

Hazel seemed nervous about the whole thing but didn't say anything. The rest of the day was awful for Molly. The girls acted as if she was no longer their friend. At lunch Amber and Hazel pretended like Molly didn't even exist! Just the day before everything had been great.

Molly decided to talk to her parents about it. The parents of all three girls knew each other pretty well, so maybe they would know what was going on. Her parents said to give it a little time and see how things went the next day. The next day was an exact repeat of the one before.

To make things worse, Hazel gave Molly a message. Amber ordered Molly to stay in the gym bathroom and not show her face until the school day was over. Molly did exactly that because she feared Amber. She cried the entire time. For two days Molly was humiliated, resulting in her feeling lonely and ashamed.

Some Questions

1. Why do you think some people pick on other people?

2. Why do you think others join in?

3. What should Molly do?

4. Why didn't Hazel stick up for Molly?

5. Have you ever been in Molly's shoes?

6. How could you help Molly?

GIRLS AND BOYS ARE DIFFERENT

I've noticed that there are differences in the types of people who are bullied. Girl victims tend to cry or stress out more than boys. Girls who are bullied spend a lot of time on the phone or computer instead of going places. Sometimes they prefer to sleep a lot because they feel down and want to hide from the world. Boy victims, on the other hand, can seem like loners or like they're lost. They tend to spend all of their time in their bedrooms. Whether the victims are boys or girls, they can be treated the same way. They need support from their friends and the adults around them.

BECOMING A FRIEND TO YOURSELF

I know kids, especially with low self-esteem, who don't give themselves credit for being who they are. But you have to be a friend to yourself and be kind to yourself before you can expect anyone else to be kind to you.

Most of the kids I know believe they are ordinary and don't have any special talents. They don't realize their talents are their own abilities and no one else's. They don't realize that they are unique and that being unique is a good thing. Being unique is who you are, what you are, your abilities, your personality. Who else can do all these things for you but you? Even your emotions are unique. Your emotions bring your own specific needs and wants out in the open, which is why it is so crucial for you to share your emotions, especially if you are being bullied. By hiding them, you're hiding yourself from the possibilities of dealing with your feelings in the way you need to.

One of the things that kids always say to me is, "I wish I were you or could be like you." Though it may be flattering, I prefer it when kids realize that all I am doing is being myself and inspiring them to be their own selves too. Only I can be me, and only you can be you. Only you can make yourself create the life that truly makes you happy. Every kid I have gotten to know has a unique talent or personality trait or something great that stands out. But when I come to bring it to their attention, they don't agree with me.

So, especially when issues of bullying come around and enter their lives, can you just imagine what torture they add to their already low view of themselves? Maybe this is you to a tee. We can try to do everything possible to eliminate bullying, but I believe that inner strength is the power to change bad things like bullying.

If you're strong in your thoughts of yourself and act as a friend to yourself— supporting who you are or who you want to be and how you want to live your life—dealing with bullying is just that, dealing with it. Lack of confidence allows kids to not even realize that the bully's power is fake. The power to deal with bullying is within you and only you. So every single day of your life, work on liking yourself first before you can like anybody else.

• •

"If you have no confidence in self, you are twice defeated in the ways of life. With confidence, you have won even before you have started."

—MARCUS GARVEY

• •

Do you ever think you're less than perfect? Everyone is born perfect. Perfect for each of us. What is perfect for you is not what is perfect for someone else. We get into trouble when we look at others and think that their perfect should be our own. Don't try to be perfect; instead try to be the best you can be. That includes acceptance of your faults, acceptance of your regrets, acceptance of bad decisions, and acceptance that bullying and bullies exist.

We already know bullies are about fake power. Victims are about real power because they're using real solutions to a fake problem. Not that bullying is fake, but its power is fake because bullies steal the victim's power to use it as their own. It's like they are aliens from another planet who can't breathe on their own, so they need to steal humans' oxygen source to survive.

So why would you give something away that belongs to only you? Why would you want to let it go, especially to a person or people who are stealing it from you? If it has happened to you already and you have let go of your power to bullying, it's time you get it back. It's been away somewhere, being used and abused by others, but your power will still recognize you if you summon it back. No matter how much time has passed or how much pain it has caused, once you rediscover your power it will be a force within you that you will have forever.

So let me ask again, do you ever think you're unique, talented, helpful, sincere, honest, genuine, loving, peaceful, compassionate, loyal, humble, or any other wonderful words you can think of? If you answered yes to any one of these, you have power. So start adding to the list of great things about yourself, one by one, day by day, piece by piece.

I'm a kid just like you. If I can do anything, you can do anything you set your mind to. Be strong, be cautious, but always be you. Hold your head up high, even when you feel defeated. As long as you know yourself well enough, you will be able to rule your world; that's all you need. Soon others will take notice.

FEAR OR FEARLESS

Fear is not real. It is something we create in our minds. So, when a bully comes at you, the fact that you don't know what is going to happen—will you be hurt, will he strike, will you be embarrassed, outed, etc.—is where your fear is coming from. You literally fear the unknown.

Here's the good news about fear. Because it's something we create, it's something we are capable of destroying. The best way that I have found to do this is to visualize the unknown, which then prepares you for the worst-case scenario and desensitizes you to it. It's sort of like injecting the flu into your system to prevent the flu during flu season. You insert the bad hypothetical outcome and it basically makes you immune to its power. And that's the way to becoming fearless.

When you're in school and suddenly feel worried or scared about something, remember the fear is only living in your thoughts. But since you control your thoughts, you can redirect them to control your fear. So my theory is, you need to become aware at that moment that you have total control to lead your thoughts. Fear is fake, and the greatness is that you can turn it into a real positive exploration of your own mind that no one can ever control, except you. When you present yourself as fearless to a bully (even if you're faking it), guess what? The bully can't handle it, not one bit. You've just become fearless. How does it feel?

BYSTANDER, BYSTANDER!

Most of the time, bullying occurs when a teacher or adult isn't around. Bullies wait until the people with authority are gone. With no one to stop them, they use their false power against their victims. But even if an adult doesn't see a bully in action, usually someone else does.

> "When a bystander gets involved, there's a good chance that bullying will decrease or stop entirely."

A person who sees a bully picking on someone else is a bystander. The bystander is the key to helping people stay safe. When a bystander gets involved, there's a good chance that bullying will decrease or stop entirely.

Special Victims

Gay, lesbian, disabled, and overweight kids are victims more often than other kids. And now there is even a new term used to make fun of kids with red hair—"gingers." These days anybody with so much as a freckle could be considered a freak. But all of these people are just like everyone else! They can grow up to be your doctor or your teacher or your leader. They can become parents and coaches and scientists and actors.

SUCCESS STORY: MEET ROBERT

When I was younger, one of my classmates was a boy named Robert. I liked him a lot because he was very nice and caring. But that didn't matter to the other kids. Every day they laughed at him and called him "gay" to his face. I was a *bystander* to this bullying, and every week Robert grew sadder and sadder. Eventually he got to the point where he almost didn't talk at all.

Every day I went home and talked to my parents about Robert. Finally, I began to stand up for him. That's what bystanders should do—stand by a victim's side. I told the other kids that he was my friend and that they should leave him alone. I also invited him to hang out with me during lunch and had him over to my house to swim.

Everyone at school backed off and left him alone. On my birthday all my friends came over, including Robert. He brought me a bouquet of flowers! I knew I had made the right choice to take action instead of stand around and do nothing. Years later he moved away, but we're still friends.

Sometimes, though, we let these meaningless things get in the way. Let's say that two people are hidden behind a curtain. The thinner friend is very intelligent. So is the obese friend. The thinner friend gives you respect and support. So does the obese friend. The thinner friend can't promise to always have your best interest at heart but the obese friend can.

You must choose between the thinner person and the obese one. The trick is that you can't see what they look like. Which one will you pick? I can tell you without a doubt which one I would pick. I would pick the one who will be a true friend, one I can count on no matter what. In this case, that happens to be the obese one.

Most people who couldn't see the two people would make the same choice. The minute the curtain rises, though, a lot of people will immediately change their minds. They would rather have the thinner friend, because they have been influenced by the media and magazines. Those kinds of people don't deserve the true friend!

NO WAY OUT

For years Jacob had been bullied by a bunch of other boys because he had learning disabilities. The bullies would call him names and tell him that he was a freak and he should go to another school because he wasn't wanted in theirs. Everywhere he went he saw one or more of the bullies. They took every opportunity to treat him poorly. They laughed at him and held up their fists as if they might hit him. It didn't matter where Jacob went or what he was doing; the bullies were always around.

One day, the group began shouting that he should go kill himself. He couldn't handle it anymore. He crunched up into a ball in the corner and started to cry. He actually thought about killing himself. If he couldn't get away from those boys, maybe killing himself was the only answer.

Another boy noticed all the mean things the group had been doing. He didn't know Jacob, but he told a teacher what was going on. The adult wasted no time looking into the situation. The bullies were written up and warned to stop harassing Jacob. That was all it took. None of the boys ever bothered Jacob again!

After dealing with depression for a long time, Jacob had become overwhelmed. When someone is hurt like that, day after day, and no place seems safe, kids might think that the only way to end the bullying is to end their lives. But that is just not the truth! Suicide is the third leading cause of death among teens, behind accidents (first) and homicide (second).

There are other ways to stop the pain. It's important for kids who have never been bullied to know how awful victims feel and to report things to adults because you never know when you might be saving someone's life, just through the simple act of telling. Nobody even has to know that it was you who told. Have you ever seen the sign at the airport about spotting terrorists: "If you see something, say something"? Well, if you see someone being terrorized by a bully, say something.

> *"If you see something, say something."*

CALLING ALL VICTIMS

Have you ever been a victim of a bully? I've included some questions here for you to answer to help you answer this question. You may be being bullied and don't even know it or realize it. This can happen to anyone at any time because of not being able to recognize that it is happening. It might come to your mind to ask yourself "Am I being bullied?" but you may be afraid of the answer being yes, and therefore, continue to accept bad being done to you. So, here you might be able to find out what's really happening in your life. For example, anyone who keeps pressuring you to do something you don't want to do is bullying you. For instance, if you don't like ballet and would rather sign up for soccer because you have brothers and have always played soccer with them, you enjoy doing it, and feel confident to try out, but the person you call your friend is constantly feeding you things like "Soccer is a boy sport," "I've seen you play and you're not very good," "You're only going to disappoint the team and yourself for doing it," or "You really need to try ballet and act like a girl," that's bullying!

Anyone who acts like your friend when you're alone with them but puts you down and embarrasses you when there is a group of kids around is a bully. Anyone who claims that constantly bumping, pushing, or tripping you is always an accident is a bully. One time might be an accident, two times could be a coincidence, but after that, it is terrorizing and on purpose.

Knowledge is power. I'm a believer in "The more you know, the better you will do when making decisions about right and wrong." Answering the questions on pages 48–49 will help you to keep your power. And by the way, when thinking about answering these questions, keep in mind that bullying can happen not only by your peers but also by a parent or other adult. Sometimes bullies never grow out of their ugliness.

SPOTTING SUICIDE

People who are thinking about suicide might give out warning signs in hope that they will be rescued. If you see any sign that someone is that sad and overwhelmed, you must take action, and fast! Don't be afraid to get help for yourself or someone else. Ask about the kinds of help that might be available. Suicide is preventable, so act quickly.

Some warning signs are:

- Hopelessness
- Desperation
- Anxiety
- Sleep problems
- Increased alcohol and/or other drug use
- Recent impulsiveness and taking unnecessary risks
- Threatening suicide or expressing a strong wish to die
- Making a plan:
  - Giving away prized possessions
  - Sudden or impulsive purchase of a firearm
  - Obtaining other means of killing oneself, such as poisons or medications
  - Unexpected rage or anger

(Source: American Foundation for Suicide Prevention)

Some other warning signs of potential suicide victims are:

• Someone who is usually friendly and outgoing might stop returning calls or stop talking altogether like my friend Robert did.

• A drastic drop in grades. Even if someone isn't the best student to begin with, a big drop can signal big problems.

• Talking about suicide. Even if someone seems to be joking, pay attention! It may be a cry for help.

The number to National Suicide Prevention lifeline is 1-800-273-8255. Please call if you need help.

(Source: www.suicidepreventionlifeline.org)

1. Has anyone ever called you inappropriate names?

2. Has anyone ever shoved, pushed, or touched you in an aggressive way?

3. Have you ever been threatened? Threats are a big thing for bullies.

4. Has someone ever said something mean about your appearance?

5. Do you feel like people are sarcastic to you often?

6. How often do you see people being bullied in a typical school day?

7. How important is your image to you?

8. Do you feel that you don't have any friends?

9. Are you constantly teased? What do they say to you?

10. Are your grades dropping?

11. Do you feel alone?

12. Do you feel aggression but don't understand why?

13. Do you feel worst at home than you do at school?

14. Have you seen your parents bully each other?

15. Have you felt belittled by your parents?

16. Do you feel that your siblings hate/or want to hurt you?

For any of these questions, answering them as honestly as possible will help you find that you may have more than one issue. When deciding if you

"Knowledge is power."

should tell anybody, ask yourself, "What is the biggest fear stopping me?" More than likely many other people share the fear, so you are never alone. Did you tell anybody about what you were feeling or going through? Why or why not? Making the decision is not about telling somebody; it is about sharing. You will find that sharing is the key to unlock fear. You could find many reasons why you would rather not tell anybody and you could find one reason why you should tell somebody. The one reason is enough to take the step to speak up. Speaking up gets easier each and every time you do it. If you're not ready today, don't give up. Try again tomorrow.

YOU DON'T HAVE TO REMAIN A VICTIM OF BULLYING

It's true! So you have been a victim of bullying for way too long, and you're feeling stressed, weak, scared, and in some extreme cases, suicidal. It is your reality, but your reality can be a different reality today than it was yesterday. This is sometimes a crazy world, and it may feel so out of control about what you're supposed to have control over. Well guess what? You control your thoughts and your reactions to every action.

Most people are afraid to get out of their comfort zone, leaving no room to take risks. Kids feel that their comfort zone means fear can't touch them. The comfort zone also means that they don't have to face bullies. But you must get out of your comfort zone. You must face the bully; you must deal with the scary feelings, because the "safety" you feel will only be short term. Why do I say this? Because letting go of anything bad is worth taking a risk. Easier said than done—well, that's the only way. Because I know you don't want to stay a victim of bullying, I know you don't want to be treated badly, and I know you're sick and tired of it.

When the bully comes around, the problem usually is that you don't know what to say to them. Say this very loud and clear, straight to their face, and it's best if other people are around, "I don't let people like you get to me!" or "You are a waste of my time." Practice saying it, until you're ready to say it. Practice makes perfect. When you say it, walk away, never leave room for confrontation; go and tell someone what happened. I guarantee you, when you do this, you'll feel like a brand-new you.

The point you want to get across to the bully is you don't want to argue, you don't want to win the battle, because a battle takes two and you're not willing to battle. Your only job is to let the bullies know that you don't have the time, the need, or the desire to be involved in their issues. But you still want to make it clear that you have a voice. And your voice will be heard loud and clear.

Keep remembering: bullies are all about hurting you because they have so much hurt themselves. They release it out to the open, wanting it to hurt others as well. After all, misery loves company! A voice with meaning and substance will win over the voice with a hurtful mission. But remember not to limit your voice just to yourself; use your voice to help others.

MIRROR, MIRROR

Being bullied warps your confidence and makes you believe false things about yourself. You must remember who you are and that your bully's words and actions do not define you.

One exercise you can do every day to keep your mind free of the things that clutter confidence is use a mirror. In the morning as you get ready for school, think about yourself in good ways. Look in the mirror and tell yourself, "You matter," "You're unique," "Mean kids will not get you down today," or "I have the world in front of me. Today is just the beginning." Whatever comes to you from your gut about who you believe you are, what you are capable of doing, what kind of person you want to be, or the changes you want to make in the world, say it in the mirror. For real impact, when you get ready for bed each night, repeat the same exercise.

The exercise is so easy that you can do it anytime. Once you start, you'll be surprised how often you can squeeze a few good thoughts about yourself into your day. Like anything, you do need to practice this exercise. If you don't, you won't get as much benefit out of it.

SHANAYA'S SHORT LIST

- Bullying is always intentional.

- Bullying is never an accident.

- Bullying happens over and over.

- Bullying is false power.

- Bullying can come from an individual or a whole group of people.

- Bullying is not a game.

- Bullying is wrong.

- You don't have to tolerate bullying!

SETTING YOURSELF FREE—HOW TO TELL

If you want to talk to your parents or grandparents or other guardian about being a victim yourself, start by making a list of what you want to say. Be sure to identify your fears. Then set a time to talk. Don't do it at dinner-time or when the adult is distracted.

Before you talk, take deep breaths. Use your list to keep you on track. You might read it like a speech. When you are done, let your parents talk even if you don't like what they say. Your parents might say something like, "Get over it, everybody goes through it." Or "Figure it out yourself. I can't do it for you." Hold back any anger and avoid feeling too much frustration. Thank them for listening.

If your parents decide to help, tell them they have made the right decision. Even if they decide not to help, use the opportunity to build trust. Never throw fits because they won't help you. Instead go to your room and write down your feelings. You can also go outside to take a walk or run around the block. The exercise will help you calm down and get rid of all your stress!

My school presentations usually run thirty to sixty minutes long. But for any of my ideas to have a real impact, bullying needs to be addressed each and every day. Teachers need training so they can handle bullying as it occurs. Parents are responsible for teaching life lessons at home.

Every adult has to become part of the solution!

3

Cyberbullying

When I spoke at a school recently, I met with students in person during lunchtime. A lot of them told me their stories of being bullied or how their friends were bullied. One boy, who was new to the school, asked if I could help him. I gave him one of my business cards so he could call me after school and share his story.

It was awful. He'd been getting emails filled with comments about how ugly he was. The emails also said that some of the students were going to beat him up. Because of an illness he had for many years, he wasn't physically strong or prepared to defend himself. And, since his father was working in a different country, the boy didn't feel like he could talk to his parents about it.

I finally convinced him to talk to his mom. I also suggested that he delete his email address and create a new one. Then, with his permission, I spoke to his mother. I let her know that she could prove to the school administration that her son was being cyberbullied by letting them see the emails. Once they know about the situation, they could address the problem.

The last time I spoke to that boy, he seemed better. He wasn't getting all those awful emails anymore and had even started going out to the movies.

Telling is often difficult, I know, because you don't want to seem weaker in the eyes of your bullies. I have heard a lot of stories about bullying getting worse because someone was being thought of as "running home to mommy," but in the end, you have to have the *courage* to take your chances. There is a chance your bullying could get worse, but there is an equal chance that it could get better! It takes courage to find out. If your bullying gets worse, at least now you have a support system or friends and adults who know what is happening and how you feel and you won't feel alone. Feeling alone and helpless and unloved is what causes depression and anxiety. Don't be alone. Just tell someone.

CYBERBULLYING

Here is a checklist for parents and kids to use when going to authorities.

VICTIM:

Name_____ Date of Birth _____

Address_____

Attending School_____ Grade_____

Parents' Phone Numbers _____

BULLY:

Name_____ Age (if known) _____

Attending School (if known) _____

Date of Incident _____ Location_____

Explanation of Occurrence Against the Victim _____

_____

Witnesses_____

Parents_____

If School(s) Was Notified ❑ Yes   ❑ No

If Yes, Name of the Contacted School Official _____

Signature of Victim   _____

Signature of Witness(s)_____

Signature of School _____

Signature of Parent/Guardian_____

WHAT IS CYBERBULLYING?

Remember when I said all bullies are cowards? Well, cyberbullying proves it. Out there in the electronic world, people can't see you and might not know your real name. Bullies hide behind that cyber curtain. As long as they stay hidden, they think they hold power over their victims.

Cyberbullying is a huge part of the bullying problem. Any kind of bullying hurts, plain and simple. The victim's pain doesn't feel any less awful just because the bullying happens over email. It can even seem worse, though, because the victim might not know who's on

"Don't be alone. Just tell someone."

the other end. They wonder if their friends might be the bully. If they become too paranoid, they cut themselves off even from people who love them!

Cyberbullying comes in many forms. It includes any kind of electronic messages like emails, texts, instant messages, and postings on social networks. The key is that it doesn't happen face to face. The victim never sees the bully, but the words cut just as deep. And the really scary part is that this stuff stays out in the cyber world forever. So, it's not as easy for a victim to get away from, even years later. Sometimes, it can follow you to your first job!

If you know people who are cyberbullying ask them if they would like their spiteful, poor behavior to follow them for the rest of *their* lives. They can easily not get into a college of their choice or another private program if their name and background is researched enough to discover how cruel they were when they were kids. Now, *that's* food for thought.

SOCIAL MEDIA "FRIENDS"

A study that was conducted by Pew Research Centers Internet and American Life Project found that social media use is widespread among teens. Ninety-five percent of twelve- to seventeen-year-olds in the survey said they use the Internet. Of those, 80 percent reported they use social-media sites. When it comes to bad conduct online, 80 percent of teen social media users in the survey said they have defended a victim of meanness and cruelty, and 79 percent said they have told someone to stop bad behavior on a social networking site.

The disturbing part is that 21 percent said they have joined in on the terrible harassment. Teens are mean to each other on social-media sites because there is a sense of protectiveness and being invisible, even though you're not.

As everyone should be aware, adult bullies exist as much as kid bullies do. I have had many adults say negative things about me in the past and even had an adult bully! For me, I realized that my adult bully was jealous of my success and let it get the best of him. Jealousy can be a big reason to bully someone.

My story began when an adult, after finding out that I had recorded a single and music video, began to basically stalk everything and anything I said or posted. If I posted, for example, that I was graduating high school years earlier than my peers, he would almost immediately post bad, crude, and disrespectful remarks that were in relation to my post. He became so out of hand that I finally had to delete him from my friends list and block him from everything. But what I have learned is, the more I do and the more successful I become, the less support I get.

I am very fortunate and grateful to the support system in my social-media outlets, which continues to support me 100 percent, but it is a small group and I can name each one of them. And they make everything else meaningless.

Everyone needs support in one way or another, and it's not all going to be at the same time; some need it sooner and some need it later. Social media can be a good thing for growth and for learning about each other and making new friends along the way. So if you ever encounter meanness, direct or indirect bullying, or explicit content, it just takes blocking and reporting to get away from it quickly.

Social media has its fault in that people feel free to work out their anger or frustrations over the Internet. If there is something you have to say or if you're angry with someone, there are ways to talk about it with him or her through a private message in a calm and friendly manner. And the same goes if someone sends you something disturbing. Even if you think it is not that big of a deal, it actually might be, so don't deal with it alone or allow it to get out of hand. Don't share it so that you can grab a bunch of people's attention and turn it into a lynch mob.

There used to be a time when you would get home from school and feel safe from bullies. But it's no longer that simple. Bullies go with you even to your safe place now through social media, and they can even be adults.

SUCCESS STORY: MY CYBERBULLY

If you've seen me speak, you might think that I'm too confident to be a victim. You might watch me walk across the stage and speak to hundreds of students without looking nervous or scared. How could someone who can do that be bullied? Well, I have been bullied more than once. Bullies are everywhere and they can attack anyone!

One of my experiences happened at the beginning of the school year. I had known a friend I'll call Allison for about two years. We spent a lot of time together, and Allison even spent the night at my house a few times. After those nights, I noticed that many of my things were missing. *Was Allison stealing from me?*

At some point, Allison invited another girl, Savannah, over to her house. Savannah was friends with both of us and had been to my house plenty of times. Savannah saw many of my things in Allison's room.

When I asked Allison about it, she denied taking anything. I told her that our friendship was over. Until she could be honest and apologize, I didn't want to talk to her. After about a day, she called. She was crying hysterically and asked me to forgive her. She admitted to taking most of the things.

After thinking carefully about what had happened, I

realized that Allison had never been my friend. Friends should love each other and help each other. They should never steal from each other! I decided to put this friendship on the backlist. I would be nice to her if we had a class together, but I wasn't going to let her hurt me again.

Then the bullying started. She kept calling, and I don't mean once in a while. She called twenty or thirty times a day! I didn't answer the phone when her number showed up so she left messages on my voicemail. After a while I had to change my phone number.

A few months later, I went to the social network I use for encouraging an anti-bullying program. That Friday night I asked everyone in the network to post their thoughts on bullying. Saturday morning I found a post from Allison. I didn't want to believe what she'd written!

Shanaya, no one is interested in listening to you because you don't have any real friends like I do. People don't want to help you, you're always bothering everyone, and you should stop it!

Although she had waited months to post, the comment was really about the fact that I wouldn't be her friend. She had probably been keeping up with the networking site all that time. She'd hidden behind the cyber curtain until she could attack!

I knew exactly what to do. First, I took a deep breath and slowly let it out. That helped me to relax, which meant I could think clearly. I told myself that her post wouldn't hurt me. When you're under attack, it's important to remember that a bully's words mean nothing. Never give hate any power!

Then I had to make sure she couldn't attack me again so I removed her from my network. Finally, I had to do something about the post. As long as it was up, many people could read it. They might worry about me or be afraid to post their own comments in case Allison attacked them! So I clicked the delete button next to her post. Allison and her meaningless words went away. It was that easy.

> *"When you're under attack, it's important to remember that a bully's words mean nothing. Never give hate any power!"*

If you ever wonder whether someone is a true friend, it must be for a reason. In any friendship, trust is a must! Trust is the core of friendship. It cannot be broken. Many times you will feel it in your gut that something just isn't right. I am the type of person who believes in forgiveness, but something about Allison's behavior just didn't sit right with me. Trust your gut; it will never let you down.

DEALING WITH CYBERBULLYING

Some kinds of cyberbullying might be a lot tougher to handle than what I went through. If you start getting emails or texts or posts that are filled with hate, think carefully about how to handle them. You might ask a parent or someone you trust for help. Having another person back your decision can give you the confidence to stop the bully. It all starts with taking that deep breath though. It's key because it helps you not fire off something you'll regret or make a big deal out of something that is pointless, like the bully's words.

Some people might be too embarrassed to admit that someone is bullying them. They worry that people will think they did something wrong to make the bullying start. That's *never* true. Don't ever think that asking for help will show you in a bad light. Being bullied in any form is not your fault!

"Being bullied in any form is not your fault!"

No matter how serious your situation might be, never lash out at the bully. Don't send hateful emails and don't post nasty comments. That only feeds the bully's behavior. They know they got you where they want you, highly emotional and stressed out. That makes them feel powerful over you. Don't play their game. If you want to beat them at their own game, ignore them. It will make them feel silly and look foolish to themselves and anybody else they're trying to impress. They know that you will lash out if you're hurt, and that just makes them do even worse things! Instead, take back your power by looking for a real solution.

Talk with parents or friends about different ways to deal with the cyberbully. Go to the authorities at your school. Call in the bully's parents because they probably don't know what's going on. You don't have to follow every suggestion your parents or friends make. In the end, though, you're the one who has to get out of the bad situation. And it's best to do that as quickly as possible!

THE TEXT BULLY

I'm going to tell you about a friend I'll call Maya. We'd known each other for about four years, so I thought our friendship was solid. Even though I felt some doubts, I invited Maya to spend the night at my house a few times. Back then, I tended to accept people even when I felt something wasn't quite right.

The last few times we got together, she spoke to me in a mean tone. That isn't how friends should treat each other, so I told my mom I was thinking about not being friends with Maya anymore. I decided to trust my gut. I no longer enjoyed being around her and ended the friendship.

The next week I received a text message from Maya. It said that I needed to call her ASAP. I was on my way to a youth council meeting, so I texted back that it wasn't a good time. When she responded, she seemed to have lost her mind! It read:

You're not the only ***** who is ******* busy!

Well, I didn't have to think too long about how to handle that! The best way was to not respond at all. Her text was just wrong, and I wasn't going to feed her classless behavior by lashing out or trying to calm her down. She wanted attention, but she wasn't going to get it from me!

Two weeks passed. Then one of my online friends asked if I knew what Maya had been doing to her. Maya had been posting things like:

Stop being a crybaby just because I have thirty friends and you have zero friends, ha, ha, ha. All you do is cry like a baby and if you, Shanaya, see this, mind your own business!

Soon after that, another on-line friend sent me a message. The things Maya had been doing had gotten so bad they had started to feel like cyber-stalking! This second girl had been forced to defriend Maya. She had actually closed her account and opened a new one.

But in the end, we found out who our true friends were and ended the stalking. I hadn't lost a friend; I had gained some pride. The same can happen to you, if you just stay calm and smart about things, and listen to your instincts. They are what hide in your gut.

4

How to Help

When I was in fifth grade there was a girl in my class named Samantha. She always seemed so sad. At lunchtime, a group of kids was teasing her about the size of her hips. She tried hard not to cry, but she teared up. I walked over to her table and introduced myself. I wasn't sure what to do but thought anything was better than nothing, so I asked if she wanted to eat with me outside. She seemed relieved and thanked me over and over again.

I had to take care of some other things before lunch ended so I left. I walked back into the classroom a little early. Samantha was already there. Her head was on her desk, and she was crying hysterically. No one in the room seemed even a little concerned. I flat out asked if I could do anything to help. Still crying, she kept repeating that no one liked her.

For days after that, she completely shut down. She wouldn't talk to anyone, she didn't do her school work, and she often had crying spells. One morning she was waiting for me at the front door to the school. She asked if I would walk with her. When we got to the classroom, Samantha asked the teacher if she could move her desk closer to mine.

Somehow that made her feel better. I'm sure she also felt safer. No one bothered her when I was around! Despite that, the next few weeks were very dramatic. Samantha's grades dropped severely. Though everyone knew I would protect her, even the people bullying her felt that they were unable to bully me.

Over time, I tutored her on weekends. It wasn't easy, but that motivated her to do her schoolwork again. By the end of the year, she had gained enough confidence to get back on track. She had even gained the respect of the other students. Many kids actually became her friends.

- -

WHAT WOULD YOU DO?

Situation
A new girl starts school late in the year. She doesn't know anyone and is always alone. During lunch, you notice that she sits at a table far from everyone else. She looks sad and lonely. What do you do?

Situation
While walking through the halls, you see some of your classmates teasing a new boy. They act like they're trying to get to know him by asking questions about where he's from. But every time he answers, they make mean jokes about what he says. What do you do?

- -

PEER PRESSURE, BULLY STYLE

A boy I heard about was very good at sports. Michael was so good that he wanted to play on a high-level team in another state. He moved in with a family his parents knew really well and started playing on the school team.

Right from the start, a bully picked on Michael because he was Jewish. It wasn't long before he was being treated the same way by many of his teammates.

The situation got so bad he quit sports and went back home.

In this case, a bully pressured other people into attacking Michael. Sometimes we know it's wrong to do something, but we do it anyway. It might be something small like taking an extra carton of milk off the lunch line. Or it might be something big like going along with a bully.

Going along with a bully doesn't mean that you push someone or call them names. If one of your friends bullies someone, you might laugh at the victim or cheer your friend on. Either way, you have taken on a bad role.

When you are with your friends, you won't always agree with things they say or do. Most of the time you don't say anything because you're afraid of losing their friendship. But when you have a bully for a friend, you're going to be pressured to say or do things you know are wrong. Even if you only watch, by not taking action you're helping the bully. In fact, you are being bullied yourself.

Remember that bullies like to feel like they have power over other people. They might not be mean to you, but at some point they'll want you to do what they do. The pressure is another kind of power that is false, like they begin to think they are the leader. Simply don't do anything you don't want to! It's much better to lose that friend if they are always trying to involve you in bad behavior, and gain your pride.

BEAT THE BULLY'S GAME

If you find yourself being pressured to help a bully, there are lots of things you can do. The simplest one is to walk away. You always have the power to make your own

> *"If your friends try to get you involved in bullying, find other friends!"*

choices. Take a minute to think about who will benefit from your actions—you or the bully? If your friends try to get you involved in bullying, find other friends!

Sometimes you might get pressured into doing a few small things that are wrong. You might watch your friend bully someone and not say anything. You might also laugh at a mean comment before you figure out what's going on. If that happens, realize that you've made a mistake. We all make mistakes!

Don't feel guilty about your past. As long as you don't do it again, you're making the right choice. Keep doing what you know is right and you'll take the power back from the bully. If you still feel bad about your mistake, talk to your parents or a teacher. You can also talk to a friend you trust. Once you feel better about yourself, you won't be pressured into making that mistake again.

WHAT WOULD YOU DO?

Situation
During PE class, everyone goes outside. The biggest boy in your grade pushes another boy into a puddle of mud. The gym teacher didn't notice because he was talking to another teacher. What do you do?

Situation
One of your best friends starts spreading rumors about your other best friend. You find out that they got into a fight earlier that week. What do you do?

STAND UP AND BE HEARD

Making the right choices can be hard. It's not fun to think about losing friends, especially ones you've known for a long time. But sometimes friends change. They don't feel good about themselves so they start to bully other kids. They want you to be a bully, too, because that makes them feel even better!

Feeling good about hurting other people is wrong. Staying out of that bad behavior is simple, but it sure seems difficult. If you take a little time to think things through, you can be prepared for when it happens.

It is your job to learn lessons that will help you be successful, productive, and caring. This is the minimum you should accomplish as you're growing up. It will allow you to do what you truly love and to share that with others. The best way to reach this goal is to be kind to your friends and family. You have the ability to make your dreams a reality! Whenever you have a problem, try sleeping on it before making a decision. Use positive thoughts to change your behaviors. If you ever feel like you're in danger, trust yourself. You are your own best friend. Everyone else is second in line!

Here are just a few ways bystanders can help stop bullying.

❖ Discourage the bully before anything happens, like if your gut says to you that there is going to be some kind of confrontation, let someone at the school know so that there could be an intervention.

❖ Intervene when bullying starts. Even if you are not sure what you are going to do once you get there, like when I went to the table to save Maya from the teasers, your presence will tell them that they are not in control. You are!

✣ Defend the victim. Whether you take her out of the situation or just tell the bully to stop, your defense will make a big difference. Learning the defending lines in the next chapter will be really handy, too.

✣ Change the situation. Just like Maya had her desk moved next to mine, there is always a creative solution to change the situation.

✣ Call on the victim's friends for support.

✣ Report the bully to a teacher, counselor, or principal. This has an enormous positive impact!

5

Take Action

Jason was the neighborhood bully. Unfortunately, Sam lived next door to him. Although Jason wasn't very big, he'd been picking on Sam for years. Every time Sam played basketball or soccer, Jason took the ball. Sometimes he pulled at Sam hard enough to tear his clothes. Sam always ended up crying and going back inside.

One day Sam was shooting hoops. Jason shoved him hard enough to knock him down. Well, this time was once too many! Sam went inside and let Jason think that he'd won again. A few minutes later, he went back outside and found Jason sitting on a stone wall outside his house.

"The next time you give me crap," Sam said, "I won't take it anymore!"

Jason started laughing. He picked up a rock and threw it right at his face. That was it! Sam grabbed Jason's legs and yanked him off the wall. He dragged him down the sidewalk nearly half a block. The whole time Jason screamed for help. Sam finally stopped and looked down. Jason was terrified.

"Please," he said, "I promise I won't hurt you. I'll give all of your balls back. Just please stop!"

Sam let go of his legs. "Bring all my balls back now!" he yelled.

Jason ran as if his life depended on it. He burst through the door to his house, then came out carrying a large bag filled with the balls.

"So when you feel strange around someone, it's really important to trust what you feel."

"Thank you," Sam said. "Now, if you start being nice to me, maybe we can play one-on-one sometime."

Jason gave Sam a crooked smile. "Thanks," he said.

These days Sam and Jason are always at the park's basketball court playing rather than fighting.

Success Story: Meet Becky

Becky was in the seventh grade when a bully came after her. Things started at volleyball practice. The team's best player was Armida. Becky wasn't playing well that day and kept missing the chance to spike the ball over the net.

Every time she missed, Armida gave her an angry look. After a while, Becky was pretty scared, but she tried hard not to show it. When practice was over, Armida and five other girls followed Becky home. Suddenly Armida attacked from behind. Becky did her best to protect herself. When they separated, Becky looked her right in the eye.

"I am not afraid of you," she said. "You don't scare me."

Even though Armida hadn't said anything during volleyball practice, Becky had known something was wrong. Sometimes you meet someone and feel like you've been best friends forever. Other times you meet someone and don't feel comfortable. You can't say exactly why, but things just don't feel right. Most of the time, those feelings are telling you something important.

Those feelings come from your instincts. They help guide us, and we don't even have to think about them. As we grow up, our instincts get stronger. So when you feel strange around someone, it's really important to trust what you feel. You can develop your instincts by studying exactly how you feel in different situations.

YOUR RIGHT TO DEFEND YOURSELF

Sometimes bullies go beyond words to pushing, hitting, punching, and kicking. If you are attacked physically, you have the right to defend yourself. If you do nothing, you might be hurt more seriously. No one has the right to attack you. You have the right to fight back!

The martial arts are a great way to prepare. Don't worry about how difficult it looks. With a good instructor, you'll be surprised how easy it is to learn. All you have to do is practice. If you are ever attacked, your body will know exactly how to protect itself.

The kind of martial arts I learned is Tae Kwon Do, which teaches blocking and control movements called forms. Blocking forms use your arms, legs, and other body parts to deflect punches and kicks. The bully can throw all the punches he wants, but if none of them land, he's just going to get tired! A control form is a move that stops the bully from hitting again. Once your attacker sees he can't get to you, he will stop trying to hit you.

Remember that a bully's power comes from taking control away from you. If you keep control, you take away his false power!

And know that bullies who are trained in martial arts and use it on you for purposes of hurting you while you are defenseless are breaking the law! If you need to learn some techniques quickly, look into self-defense programs offered by your local police. Some schools and libraries have it too. Talk to your principal about having the police instructors teach the program after school. If you ever have to defend yourself, learn to do it safely!

Let's say you think you might become a victim of bullying. So you walk away but find out later that the person you were with is actually really nice! That doesn't mean you can't trust your instincts. It just means your instincts aren't fully developed. Practice paying attention to your deepest feelings and you'll improve. It's just like getting better at math or a sport except you are your own teacher.

Learning to be a good listener around other people will also help you make the right choices. At times, you'll hear someone say one thing when they really mean something else. You know they don't mean it because of the tone of their voice or the expression on their face. A bully's power is false and their words can be false, too. The more you listen, the more you'll learn.

It is also helpful to learn to read people's body language. Many times you can tell if someone is sad, angry, confused, or happy, just by how they stand or hold their arms. You might even be able to guess their next move, if you are really in tune with what their body is telling you.

✤ Facial signals are a dead giveaway of what someone is thinking or scheming, especially in the eyes. Bullies will stare you down or lock eyes with you, which is a message of aggression and a challenge.

✤ Attack signals like clenching a fist ready to strike and lowering the body for stability.

✤ Exposing one's chest, by opening arms wide is saying, "Go on, I dare you."

✤ Invasion of another person's space in some way or "getting in someone's face."

✤ False friendship is often done under familiarity where you act as if you are being friendly and move into a space reserved for friends but without being invited. This gives the other person a dilemma of whether to repel a friendly advance or to accept dominance of the other.

(Source: Changingminds.org)

Bystanders use their instincts, too. When you see someone getting bullied, you feel deeply that you want to help the victim. Your instincts tell you to reach out in some way. Every time you take action, you make your instincts stronger. Soon you'll be able to listen to your feelings and hear exactly what they're telling you every time.

THE "POOR ME" MODE

Your instincts are different from your thoughts. Your instincts guide you toward the good things in life. Your thoughts create your life. Thinking positive things leads to success. Holding good thoughts in your mind makes good things happen in your world. And that's your strongest power!

You might wonder how thoughts can change your life. Think of it this way. When you hang around with bullies, you wind up being pressured to bully others. Sometimes you end up as the victim! If you didn't hang around that person, you wouldn't be put in bad situations.

The same thing happens in your mind. When you think negative thoughts about yourself or others, everything around you turns negative. Your friends turn into backstabbers, bullies target you, and everything seems to go wrong.

The thoughts put you into a "poor me" mode. That

means you think that things will never change, that your life will always be awful and full of pain. You can change that mess into something good. Recognizing it is the first step. Once you know that you tend to be too hard on yourself, you can learn how to love yourself more. If you can think it, you have the power to think it differently. Every negative thought can become a positive one. If you can think it, you can do it.

You have to catch yourself thinking negative thoughts day after day. Every time you do, you have to replace that negative idea

"If you can think it, you can do it."

with a positive one. Let's say you get up one morning and hate how your hair looks. Then you get to school and you hate the place where you sit in class. By the time you get to gym, you think that you're terrible at sports.

Change comes in small steps. When you look at your hair, think about how shiny it is instead of the fact that it's not styled perfectly. In class, think about how awful it would be to sit back in the dark corner. And remember that gym class is about building a healthy body, not how many points you score.

All you're doing is breaking an old, bad habit. Right away, you replace it with a new, good habit. It won't happen overnight, so you might get tired of paying attention after a while. Just keep going. Since you created your bad habits, you can also create new habits.

When trying to make real change in your life, ask yourself why you should change a habit rather than just saying you would like to change it. You are more capable of convincing yourself to break a bad habit than if somebody else suggested it. In other words, when you encourage yourself, you generate your own argument, which gives you the chance to change your own mind on your own terms and in your own time. Change comes when you are truly ready to make the change. Nobody can make you do it, no matter how much they hound you or beg you or try to convince you.

According to Dr. Maxwell Maltz and his book *Psycho-Cybernetics*, it takes twenty-one days to change a habit or create a new one. That's just three weeks! So at the end of the first week, you're nearly halfway there! Keep going and soon you'll feel happier and your life will be better. Only you control your fate. What kind of life do you choose?

THINK POSITIVE

Your horizons don't grow in the shade, so get out and get some sun! If you're just indoors doing nothing,

• •

"If you have a positive attitude and constantly strive to give your best effort eventually you will overcome your immediate problems and find you are ready for greater challenges."

—PAT RILEY

• •

thinking about nothing, how are you ever going to reach your goals and accomplish them along with your journey waiting to be lived? So get up, get out, and do something about it! The stronger you make your life, the brighter you make your day. The more and more you do each day will make you stronger, wiser, and help you stop worrying about or focusing on negative people and bullies. Your brain works twenty-four hours a day, seven days a week, 365 days a year, so make a daily plan to use it in a positive way.

This means to believe that you will attract the right people into your life, find your place in the world, and feel comfortable in your own skin. Remember earlier when I said stupidity creates more stupidity? Well, it's the same thing with positive thinking. You can actually change your brain with each positive thought you have. After some practice, you change your negative thoughts into positive ones without even trying. So, you might not consider yourself a "sunny" person now, but to have faith that it will get better and that negative people will wind up hurting themselves more than they can hurt you or anybody else will help you find the frame of mind necessary to survive and thrive during this hard time of your life.

Oh, and if you happen to be a bully, the same goes for you. You can stop being a "hater" as soon as you decide to. Nobody is keeping you feeling negatively toward others but you.

BE FAIR TO YOURSELF

Most of the time we don't even think twice about being ourselves. But if you worry that your friends won't like you or that they will judge you for being exactly who you are, you might change how you act. When you do things just to make others happy, you're not acting like your true self.

I've heard stories about girls pretending to like music they don't like or boys who wear sneakers that aren't even their style just to fit in. Others even tried to change the way they laughed because they were afraid their loud and long laugh would be looked at as annoying by others. We have all been self-conscious about one thing or another, but to actually change things that make you who you are is making you a victim before you are victimized.

You might also believe something about yourself that isn't true. You might think you're terrible at spelling just because you missed a few words on a test. You might feel like you'll never be good at art because you smudged the paint before it dried. These kinds of thoughts are false. Every time you have a false thought, you're not being fair to yourself. Having false thoughts over and over is the same as when you have negative thoughts all of the time: you start to only believe false things, and then they actually start coming true. This is called a self-fulfilling prophesy, but all you really have to remember is: *stop* believing false things about yourself!

In order to be fair to yourself, you first have to realize how often you aren't fair to yourself. I'm not talking about bad behavior; I am talking about what's in your spirit. That means your fears, your feelings, your insecurities, and even the silliness that makes you and other people happy. Silly or serious, these things add to who you really are.

When you see someone being bullied or are bullied yourself, you have a good chance to find out who you are—what you're really made of. In these situations, watch yourself. Do you feel scared of the bully, or are you angry because the bully is so mean? Do you think that an adult will believe you?

Your answers will help you look inside your spirit. If you are being unfair, you can replace that negative habit with a positive one. You might tell the bully to stop or go straight to an adult for help. The next time something happens, you'll be more likely to treat yourself well.

> *"When you see someone being bullied or are bullied yourself, you have a good chance to find out who you are—what you're really made of.*

EMPOWERMENT

Here is a form of role playing to help kids work out these kinds of insecurity issues. By acting out different ways you might react, you can prepare for the real thing. For this exercise you'll need:

✤ One person to play the bully.

✤ One person to play the bystander.

✤ As many victims as possible.

At the start of this scene, all the victims lie on the floor. They are scattered around the room while the bully stands at the middle. The bystander is at the edge of the room. The bully laughs and makes fun of the victims.

The bystander walks toward a victim. No matter what the bully says or does, the bystander ignores her. Reaching down with one hand toward a victim, the bystander says, "Let me help you up."

The victim gets up. The victim also ignores the bully and turns toward a second victim. The first victim helps that person stand. While the bully is still ranting, the second victim helps the third one; the third one helps the fourth. This repeats until all the victims are standing with the bystander.

Together, everyone turns to the bully. They don't say anything because they don't have to. By helping each other, they've said everything the bully needs to know. The bully has become an outcast.

Take a few minutes to write out your own role-playing script. Your story can be about two people or a whole class. It can take place at school or your favorite hangout. The bully can be a boy, a girl, or a group of people. Write out how people can stop bullying, and you'll really do it!

A LETTER TO YOU

Writing a letter to someone you really care about is pretty meaningful. Now you're going to write the most powerful, meaningful letter you will ever write. This letter will be written to you from you! Why? Because we forget all of the time to tell ourselves nice things. Our lives become so busy we forget who we are in the first place. Sometimes our circumstances are so confused, we become unsure about where we are heading in life. Sure, we'll tell our friend how great she is, or a dad how much he is loved, or even a coach, but what is so wrong about thinking good things about yourself and then dedicating time for you to remember and celebrate who you *really* are. Simply complimenting yourself can go a long way in building confidence and the main "C" word: courage.

Grab paper and a pen or pencil. Go to a private place. You might sit in a quiet corner of the library or go outside. Close your eyes for a few minutes. Imagine that you're in a place that makes you feel safe, comfortable, and happy. My happy place is actually in the future. I imagine that I'm an adult doing all the things I do now.

Most people will imagine a physical place. And since your imagination has no limits, the place doesn't have to be one that you've seen before. You can imagine being in Rome, Italy, or the Antarctic. Hey, maybe you can imagine the moon or the zoo. You could also make up your happy place. If you're a chocolate lover, your happy place could be a glowing world made of chocolate!

Once you're in your happy place, think about people who love you just the way you are. Then think about yourself. What will you look like in your happy place? How will you act? What will you feel inside?

Now open your eyes and start to write. Describe the self you imagined in your happy place. Don't compare yourself to how you are now; that's not what this is about! Write words filled with happiness and good feelings. Explain your inner understanding of yourself.

When you are done writing, sign the letter *Love* and your name. Be sure to date it. Put the letter in an envelope, then store it somewhere safe. Whenever you feel sad, bullied, or think that nothing is going well in your life, get the envelope. Find a private place and read your letter to yourself.

Pay attention to every word. Thank yourself for being you! Put the envelope away again. Every time you need help, read the letter again.

This simple exercise has a powerful positive impact. It won't take much time, but you'll be surprised how well it works.

SUCCESS STORY: TAYLOR

During the school year, Taylor was the victim of terrible, hurtful, malicious, and unexplainable bullying. On the last day of school a couple of mean girls followed Taylor into the restroom. The door was locked shut by a few boys who were keeping watch for the mean girls. Taylor didn't know what to do, and before she could figure out an exit, the girls attacked her.

As Taylor told me her horrific story, I could barely see her eyes from beneath her long dark bangs, and her head was down as she sat hugging herself. Her body language wreaked a lack of self-confidence. I knew the only thing I could do was give her a crash course on building self-esteem.

The first thing I told Taylor was she wouldn't be able to change the bullies, but she sure could change it from happening again. I taught her how to write a letter to herself and explained how to do the mirror exercise every morning. And more importantly how to appear to have confidence, even though she was not there yet—she could at least fake it for the time being. We listed three things she liked about herself, and made a pledge to work on the things she didn't.

About a month later, and during several contacts with Taylor, her mother contacted me to tell me that Taylor had literally transformed into a new, confident person. She stands tall, speaks up, and now reaches out to other victims.

Three Things I Like About Myself

I can't even count how many times I have heard kids say, "I don't like anything about myself." I am not convinced that's what they actually mean. What I think is that kids do like things about themselves, but lack the confidence to say it because it makes them feel embarrassed or maybe shy. Or sometimes, they think it's being boastful, which is so not true.

The following exercise will help you understand that it is okay to like yourself and shine. I'll go first by sharing three things I like and dislike about myself.

1. I am completely obsessed with learning and growing from what I have been taught.

2. I never worry about bad opinions people have of me.

3. I absolutely love my hair!

The three things I don't like about myself are:

1. I can't stop eating too much junk food.

2. I don't like to exercise.

3. I don't like sports, and I am not open to learning them.

So there you have it folks! It's as easy as that. Once you have your likes and dislikes written down, focus on the three things you like about yourself and use them to take that next step to bring excitement to you! Because life is exciting, you just have to take the time to be exciting yourself—and excited about yourself! If you can do this, you can bring excitement to everyone around you.

For example, let's start with the first one on my like list. Every day I learn something new, either on purpose or by accident. I literally feel the excitement running through my veins every time it happens, but that's just me!

Number two, honestly, not even for a single minute do I ever worry if I hear, see, or read a negative thing about me. It may seem questionable to some people, but believe me, I only focus on the positive things in life; I sometimes think I'm a little abnormal in this area, but this is *my* normal.

Number three, for me, long hair is a total must in my life. It's what makes me feel beautiful and confident. I can wear it naturally curly, I can straighten it, and I can wear it up or down. Whenever I see pictures of myself, no matter how bad my facial expression is, my hair always looks good. Again, it doesn't matter that others may not share the same opinion about my hair, because that's not the point in my liking my hair. The point is, I like it, and that's the most important thing.

Don't think that you can just stop at liking three things about yourself, because that's just three things—the starting point for you to get comfortable with the idea that it is good and normal to like yourself. I have tons of things I like about myself; we're just working our way up the list, and besides, this book is about you, not me. Every time you have something you don't like about yourself, you need to remember the

Every time you have something you don't like about yourself, you need to remember three things you do like.

three things you do like. Because you will find out the three things you like are going to almost diminish the three things you don't and eventually turn your dislike list into a minimum and end up with a long list of likes.

Now, as an example, let's talk about the things I don't like about myself. Number one, I really just like the taste of junk food, people. I really do. I am working on it by not having as much of it around the house where it is easily tempting, and the good thing about this is I get a lot of support from my mom. But on the other hand, my dad is the complete opposite. He loads the house with stuff, so what can be part of the solution? Well, I can start by asking my dad to stop. By coming to terms with this junk food flaw of mine, I found a solution. Now instead of being a thing I dislike about myself, it's more of a work in progress to change it.

Number two, my avoidance of exercise. The weird thing about this is I am a blue belt in martial arts, so I don't know what really happened from then to now . . . I even have a gym downstairs in my apartment complex, but I also know that I work a lot more so I get physically tired and then just don't do it. One solution could be to not work so late. I usually work until very late at night, and therefore I wake up a bit late in the morning. What I really need to do is switch those things around. I need to get up, get downstairs, and do it. And stop procrastinating.

Number three, my disinterest in sports, which is also a little weird, since martial arts is athletic. I don't get the obsession with team sports like football, baseball, hockey, basketball, etc. But my dad is a fanatic of sports and some of my friends are as well. So maybe if I were to be a little more open about watching a football game once in a while I could maybe learn something. It doesn't mean I will turn into a super fan, but nobody really knows what the future holds.

Why is this so important in issues with bullying? Because bullies are not born bullies; it is a learned behavior. Bullies have such negative thoughts and views of themselves that their "dislike list" is overwhelmingly longer than their "like" list. So if bullies would try to take a chance to change bad thinking, their bad behaviors will change automatically. They just have to be willing to try.

For all you bullies (or wannabe bullies) out there, this book is for you too. Start by setting small goals to work on your dislikes, then do one small thing to change each one of them. This exercise will bring you to happier and healthier place and find a way to escape ugliness.

DEFENDING LINES

I've said before that victims and bystanders should never snap back at a bully. I've also said that you have the right to defend yourself against physical attacks. Well, you also have the right to defend yourself against attacking words!

I've come up with defending lines, things you can say when a bully starts teasing or taunting you or someone else. Defending lines don't stop the bullying. Instead, they build your confidence. The fact that you

DEFENDING LINES THROUGHOUT HISTORY

I bet if you asked an adult in your life to help you think up defending lines you can use against your bully, you would find out that they already have some. Back in their day defending lines were called "comebacks." Some funny ones that I found on the Internet include:

"Sticks and stones may break my bones, but names will never hurt me." (Yeah, it's a little long, and really who plays with sticks and stones anymore?)

"You're rubber, I'm glue, anything you say bounces off me and sticks onto you." (Another long one, but then I found that it was shortened anyway to "You're rubber, I'm glue . . ." That was a smart move.)

"I know you are, but what am I?" (This one just makes me laugh.)

"Whatever." (Finally, one that I can understand!)

are fighting back at all tells bullies that they're wasting their time.

The best defending lines are short. Stay calm and speak in a normal tone of voice. Make sure that when you say these lines, you look the bully straight in the eye. I know this seems scary to even think about it, but remember that you have confidence and you know who you really are deep inside, which means you know you can do this! It will feel so good after you've tried this and see that it works. Here are just a few defending lines. Use these to help you create your own:

✤ We used to be friends.

✤ Whatever.

✤ You're really wasting my time.

✤ Your words mean nothing to me.

✤ Here we go again.

✤ Is it your goal in life to do this to me?

✤ My little brother makes me feel worse than you do.

✤ Ha! Ha! Ha!

✤ You need to grow up.

✤ I never thought you would do something like this when we were friends.

✤ Just get a life!

✤ A person like you doesn't get to me.

✤ Yeah, yeah, whatever.

✤ How would you like it if someone were to do this to you?

✤ Your opinions don't matter to me . . . sorry.

✤ I heard you, and to be honest I really don't care.

✤ Is that your best?

✤ OK, so how is that supposed to make me feel?

✤ Do I care?

✤ Go ahead and keep talking 'cause I'm not listening.

✤ You're real funny!

✤ I thought you were a good person.

✤ I'm sorry that you have nothing else better to do.

✤ I can't change what you think, so I'm not going to try.

6

Anti-bullying Teams

My experiences and the research I've done convinced me that *the key to reducing bullying is the
bystander.*

Bullies tend to do bad things when people in authority aren't around, so bystanders need to speak up for the
victim! Bystanders need to start being the authorities.
Telling somebody is not snitching. Ratting or snitching
is what people do to get someone in trouble. Telling is
what you do to get someone out of trouble.

One of the best ways to eliminate bullying is to create teams of bystanders in our schools. This chapter is all about how to set up anti-bullying teams. It's the most important part of this book!

> *"Telling is what you do to get someone out of trouble."*

THE ANTI-BULLYING TEAM

There is power in numbers. Just like the role-playing exercise that shows what could happen when a bystander helps a victim up off the floor, anti-bullying teams accomplish the same thing. It makes the bully the outcast by forming unions between victims and bystanders against the rotten activities of bullies.

The first meeting will be very exciting. Everyone should take turns introducing themselves. Talk about why an anti-bullying team is necessary and how the team can stop bullying. Point out what you like about your school and what could be better. Allow everyone to voice their own points of view. Make sure you have a teacher or other faculty member there. Maybe even a class mom. An adult should be aware of what you are trying to accomplish and help guide you in positive ways to reach your goals.

Don't forget to show enthusiasm! Kids nowadays forget to show how good they feel about the things they do. Feel free to borrow some enthusiasm from other things you do when you're not at school. Your attitude will encourage others, especially your leaders.

Everyone must fill out the form on the following pages. Learning from each other's answers is important because things that bother you might not bother someone else. The form lets you give feedback for all kinds of issues. Be sure to talk about everyone's answers. Talking is a very powerful tool, so please use it!

> *Report bullying.
> It's the right
> thing to do!*

Electing Leaders

The leadership position election process should be held during the first meeting. The positions should be:

Team Leader. The leader will organize all team meetings and activities. Must possess communication skills, be self-confident, want to serve others, and want to make positive things happen.

Special tip: It's a good idea to have backup assistant leaders. That way the team can meet even if the leader is sick or has to miss a meeting.

MY BULLY HISTORY

1. I am in the _____ grade.

2. I am: ❑ female ❑ male

3. Do you feel safe in your classrooms? ❑ yes ❑ no

4. Do you feel safe in the cafeteria? ❑ yes ❑ no

5. How safe do you feel going to and from school?

   _____

6. How safe do you feel in the hallways?

   _____

7. Have you ever been treated badly? ❑ yes ❑ no

8. How often do others say things to you
   that hurt your feelings?_____

9. Do people spread rumors about you? ❑ yes ❑ no

   How often?_____

10. Have you recently been bullied and asked for help?
    ❑ yes ❑ no

11. How often do you have lunch alone?_____

12. Do you say mean things to others? ❑ yes ❑ no

13. How often have you seen someone being bullied?

    _____

14. What have you done when you've seen a student being hit?

    _____

    _____

15. Are there gangs in your school?   ❏ yes   ❏ no

16. On a scale of 1 to 10 with 10 being the worst, how much of a problem do you think bullying is in your school?

    1   2   3   4   5   6   7   8   9   10

Messenger. Student who reports bullying activity to school authority. Must possess a good personality, be likeable and persuasive.

Student Secretary. The secretary will record what happens at the meetings and prepare a list of topics to consider at future meetings. Must possess good writing skills, good listening skills, and be organized and reliable.

The secretary should list who is elected. Those individuals should sign and date the team agreement outline sheet, making sure everybody else gets a copy.

The rest of the students should be referred to as Monitors. They will report to the messenger and assist where help is needed, basically working as team players.

Think of your team like a watch. In order to tell time, every piece of the watch must work effectively. To reduce bullying, every team member needs to do their part. When a team works properly, the actions it takes can start a domino effect. Positive change will follow and the effect will be long-lasting.

First Meeting Discussion

The team should recognize that every student is different and everyone should be treated equally. Open a discussion about:

✤ Bullying in the school

✤ Different types of bullying

✤ The effects of bullying

The meeting should then adjourn. Before everyone

leaves, the next meeting's agenda should be set. The second meeting should provide education about bullying. The information might come from this book, or team members can conduct their own research on specific issues. Each topic should be scheduled so it can be fully discussed.

Reaching Out

Students have to see the teams in action to conquer bullying in your school. When they see the teams go after bullies, students feel safe enough to share in that goal. When that happens, even students who aren't on the team can help.

Your goal is to let the victim know that you care about what happened. Tell them that they can talk freely and that the team needs information in order to help. Remind the victim that they did not deserve to be bullied and that the bully's bad behavior is unacceptable. It's also important to find out if the victim has ongoing issues with bullying.

The team should welcome anyone who wants to join. Students can be allowed to sit in on a meeting without any pressure to join until they are ready to.

Teams must set up a Help Box where students can

drop notes about their concerns anonymously. The box will be placed under administrative supervision like the counselor's office, main office, nurse's office, etc. Anything bad will be thrown out, as the messages will be reviewed with discretion. If this experiment helps just one child at a time, it makes the willingness to try it a worthy and successful effort.

A signature-collecting event can be held to demonstrate how many students support the team. This will allow the team to track its progress.

Every month, teams can set up a table during lunchtime. They can talk face to face with other students about the importance of being a bystander. Every single person in the school should be a bystander, even if not on the official anti-bullying team.

Whenever a meeting is scheduled, announce the date and time through the intercom and post information on school bulletin boards.

Midyear Agenda

Just like the student government, the anti-bullying team needs to set an agenda. An agenda outlines the topics to be discussed, the issues to be dealt with, and new things to consider in the campaign against bullies.

Most teams will meet twice a month. If your school is large or if there are a lot of issues, you might meet more often. You can also request of your principal to dedicate some time for your team to address the student body during an assembly, so they know the group exists and they can join or come to meetings to learn more. As you begin to address the bullies, make sure to discuss different hurdles or obstacles, For example, if there are no witnesses to a particular incident, credibility of the bully and the student must be used. Another example would be if the bully threatened the victim further because of reporting the incident. Checking if support is given by either parent and getting someone from the school administration to weigh in on a complicated issue must be outlined before action.

Some ways to help overcome the problems are:

- Role-play and develop skits.

- Write a progress report to the principal or other authority.

- Discuss progress of past victims.

- Share new developments.

- Alert the media about the anti-bullying team's efforts. Invite community leaders to a meeting.

❖ Provide gay, lesbian, and bisexual discrimination education.

❖ Provide education about children with physical and mental disabilities.

❖ Explain how bullying differs between boys and girls.

❖ Have a guest speaker—someone who the students look up to, maybe a local leader or successful artist or author, who can talk about their experiences in childhood with bullying.

❖ Invite me to share information about bullying!

Discuss the purpose of your team with potential members. Tell them what they'll be expected to do if they join. The whole idea is to have an enormous anti-bullying team. As time goes on, most meetings will be about specific cases. The team should also regularly schedule additional activities for outreach, teambuilding, education, and awareness. Some areas you might cover are:

❖ Alcohol and drug awareness

❖ Sexual health myths and facts

❖ Cyberbullying

- Physical bullying

- Psychological and mental bullying

- Partnerships with teachers

- Suicide education

- Guest speakers from local agencies

- Approaching a victim

- How to assess a victim

- Reporting a bully

- Recruiting members

Role-playing can help the team develop its skills. As you continue to have meetings, work up different skits to help train members in all these steps. Here's just one skit to help you get used to role-playing. You'll need:

- One student to play the victim

- One student to play the team member

- One student to play the teacher

- One student to play the messenger

ANTI-BULLYING TEAM GOALS

GOALS

- Gather school team
- Train team members
- Include teachers and administrators
- Create guidelines
- Decrease incidents of bullying
- Increase adult awareness of team activities
- Continue anti-bullying activities

PLAN

- Emphasize school safety
- Discuss mistakes
- Build communication with adults and students
- Continue training for each goal
- Develop training tools (skits/quizzes)
- Recruit new members

RESULT

- Awareness that bullying is wrong, has consequences, and will not be tolerated
- Reduce incidents of bullying

The victim approaches the team member and says he has been bullied. The team member says, "It's not your fault. You did the right thing to tell me."

The team member reports the incident to the team messenger. The messenger carries the information to the teacher. The teacher, the messenger, the team member, and the victim discuss the plan of action.

POSTERS FOR POWER

A lot of the solutions in this book encourage good behavior through communication. Good behavior should also be encouraged visually. Each student on the anti-bullying team can create a poster encouraging good behavior. With the school's permission, place them side by side in a hallway. Some slogans can act as public service announcements. Consider some of these, or have fun brainstorming your own:

✤ Bullies are foolies!

✤ Bullying is the key that opens no lock.

✤ Push swings, not people.

✤ I am FAB: Fighting Against Bullying!

❖ I took the anti-bullying pledge. (This poster can be signed by all the students who took the pledge.)

❖ Bully be gone.

❖ Courage is fire. Bullying is smoke.

❖ They don't call it BULLying for nothing.

7

Stop the Gossip

The anti-bullying team will be a powerful force in your school. It will be so powerful that bullies will try to break the teams apart. Because bullies target people who are alone, they'll look for weakness from anyone on your team. The second someone lets their guard down, the bully will charge out.

BLAH, BLAH, BLAH

Usually the attack will start as gossip or rumors. Rumors can bring down anti-bullying teams. If students get the wrong message about team members, they might not want to get involved. Remember that you are all in it together. Each one of you will have the other's back. Show the bully that you are all about strength and courage.

Bullies are pros of bad behavior. Don't let that scare you one bit. The good thing about anti-bullying teams is that the moment the program starts, it will prevent bullying. By doing all the things I've outlined in this book, you'll actually stop the gossip long before it can start.

> "Bullies are pros of bad behavior. Don't let that scare you one bit."

Gossip creates negative energy and keeps us from reaching our goals. When you use energy in a good way, you just don't have time for other people's gossip. The best way to grow is to control what you say and how you say it. Negativity makes it so much harder to enjoy life.

Sometimes you can't avoid hurtful comments. When someone you love says mean things, try not to respond immediately. That person might just be trying to vent their emotions. The comments might not be about you at all!

You don't need to accept this behavior, but you

should try to help. Wait a while before asking if everything is all right. Most of the time people are relieved after talking things out. Even if they stay mean or upset, remember that the problem is coming from them, not you.

Here is an exercise to let people practice offering positive comments. You'll need two groups with five people in each group. For three minutes, each group gives positive comments to their own members. The comments might be things like, "I watched you play volleyball yesterday and you were great!" or "That poster you made is cool."

For the second part, each person tells everyone three facts about themselves. Then the groups mix for three minutes. By the end, each member will know the other members better, and everyone will have a little more experience supporting the other members.

THE ANTI-BULLYING PLEDGE

Even if you don't have anti-bullying teams in your school, you can still take action. One way is to create an anti-bullying pledge for your classroom.

Have each student write a positive sentence that supports bully-free schools on a strip of paper. Use positive phrases! You might write things like "I pledge to be fair to others and myself" or "I have the right to defend myself." Then put all of the paper into a shoebox. Have one person pull them out, one at a time, and read each one out loud.

The entire class decides which phrase should open the pledge, which should be second, and so on. When all the phrases are arranged to your liking, you will have a finished pledge. All of the students should sign the pledge before their teacher posts it on the wall. Each month the pledge is read aloud by a different student and discussed. Feel free to add to it or revise it as you and your classmates learn more about bullying.

Here is one of my creations of a sample pledge feel free to change, add, or subtract:

Each day
I support you
You support me
Bullying ends here

TWO BULLIES, MANY CHOICES

Alexis had lots of friends. After school, she always met up with them at their favorite hangout. One day, they tried to pressure her into smoking a cigarette and drink alcohol, but Alexis refused. Some of her friends there stopped talking to her because of it. All the friends made up later except for Jessica.

At the hangout, Jessica always glared at Alexis and whispered things to other people. Soon another popular girl joined Jessica. They were both so mean that Alexis stopped going to the hangout.

Rather than giving up something she loved, Alexis could have tried a couple simple things. She could have gone to the hangout when the mean girls weren't there. She could have left as soon as she felt uncomfortable. She could have stuck with her real friends and not worried about whether the other girls liked her.

Some people in Alexis's situation might have shot the mean girls some dirty looks. That never helps. Instead, a small smile sends the message that their words just don't matter. The less bothered Alexis would seem, the less the mean girls would have attacked her.

The most important thing is for Alexis to surround herself with friends who make her feel happy. Friends are nice to be around. They never whisper about you or laugh at you. Her true friends were the ones who didn't help Jessica bully her. They might not have agreed on everything, but they weren't pressured into doing something they knew was wrong.

THE LONG-TERM PLAN

It could take some time to stop bullying. The techniques shared in the book could certainly help your personal situation a lot faster than if you didn't use them, but to really end bullying in our society on a larger scale, we need proper education, which requires time. Education is an important part of any anti-bullying program, and education comes in many forms, like research, communication, reading, and interviews, but the strongest form of education comes in the form of life lessons. They are what really teach you how to live.

Life lessons are part of the solution to bullying, because you can look back on experiences and learn from your mistakes, see where you went right or wrong, and decide whether you need to act differently in the future. Life lessons are also important because through them you can learn the true meaning of friendship. People who are friends consider what is best for each other. Honesty is part of any true relationship. Think about the people you hang out with. Are there any frenemies in your group? That's an enemy who pretends to be a friend. True friends are trustworthy. They are the people you choose to stay connected with. The

> *"People who are friends consider what is best for each other."*

reality is that bullies come in many forms and people you consider your friends can become your bullies.

When you're trying to figure out who's a true friend and who's a frenemy, ask yourself if these three simple things are present in your relationship.

1. Truth

Truth in friendship goes beyond just saying, "I'm your friend." If this friend is someone who blabs everything about someone else because she is spreading gossip, remember gossip is a form of bullying. Don't let yourself get involved with gossip just because someone who is gossiping says she's your friend. A true friend must prove to be honest, truthful, reliable, and trustworthy.

A place I have used before to go to for friendships that are inspiring and motivating without being a person-to-person friendship is called www.wittyprofiles.com. It is a place where kids can vent and express feelings freely, along with creating inspirational and funny quotes and messages. There is a chat room where kids can socialize and also ask for advice from other kids from all over the world.

If you happen to be looking to make friends outside of school and you have a talent you would like to share, consider starting your own club. I developed my own volunteer services and taught acrylic painting for two years after presenting the idea to a local bookstore. I was ten years old when I started, and I was twelve years old when it ended. I always had an average from ten to eighteen kids per class, twice per month.

2. Compassion

Having an awareness of other people's suffering means you are compassionate. I have compassion for others, which makes me able to share their feelings. Understanding when someone is in physical or emotional pain and wanting to do something about it is compassion. And if you can't help someone who's hurting, at least don't hurt them more!

3. Trust

Trust comes when friends believe that the other is going to act a certain way. Trust is closely tied to truth. You can't put a coin into a machine and get a handful of trust. Trust grows with time. Friends build trust by understanding each other's character, needs, and fears and by being truthful about all things. If you have a friendship based on trust, even when you mess up, you will trust enough in the strength of your bond to tell the truth about something you might not be too proud of.

FAILURE

There is no such thing as a kid who fails. I'd rather think that kids just didn't get it right the first time or it didn't work out that time and maybe need to try again. I bring this up because in what I do I am finding more and more parents using the word "fail" to describe something their kids didn't do well or didn't accomplish. If you could take that word and categorize it in the "bad word list," I would totally do it.

If you keep saying you have failed at something, how are you going to grasp the idea that you have many chances for do-overs and that you deserve second and third chances, until you get it right. If you didn't pass your martial arts test or didn't raise your hand to ask a question or maybe just didn't make your bed, how can "failing" describe all these things? You can never fail in defending yourself. If you have rejected the bully's means to hurt you, you passed. So stop focusing on failing and start focusing on passing.

"It doesn't matter if you try, and try, and try again, and fail. It does matter if you try and fail, and fail to try again."

—CHARLES KETTERING

SUCCESS STORY: LEARN TO EARN

When I was eight years old, I entered a national book-writing contest. It took eight weeks to write and illustrate the story. After a few months, I received a large envelope. My book had been chosen from over 3,000 entries. My story won!

On that day, I learned how to earn something. Earning something like good grades, perfect attendance, or a spot on the football team takes a lot of work. Everyone can earn something if they put in enough time and effort. Learning to earn helps you feel better about yourself. It lets you know that you are valuable. A bully can never take that away from you.

At one of the schools I attended, they taught martial arts instead of PE. I met a girl in that class named Marcella. She was a few months younger than me. For some reason, her mom always encouraged her to watch me practice my forms. Marcella barely talked but always wanted to be by my side.

That was perfectly okay with me. I told her I believed she could conquer her fears and that she was good enough to compete. I was a few ranks ahead of her so I had enough experience to know she was talented. Finally, she got up the courage to enter a competition. Marcella placed first in her rank!

She was so excited about that victory. She had never won anything before. Before the contest, she'd worked hard to perfect her forms. She'd also had to face her fear of getting up in front of all those people to be judged. In that class, Marcella learned to earn something.

Learning to earn can make a big difference for you, too. It's not about winning. Instead it's about enjoying life and having fun. And you don't have to enter competitions to earn something. You can be curious about others and listen closely to what they say. Look at their values and choose to be with positive people. You'll earn good friends and lasting relationships. You are who you are, and you *are* important whether you win or lose any competition.

Many of my friends are members of Girl Scouts or Boy Scouts, and they feel accomplished by earning badges. You are definitely in the winning circle when you volunteer what you can and to people and organizations you feel strongly about. I have volunteered to tutor in academic subjects, and have made friends in other schools by doing so. I have even taught several classes in guitar and music. One of my students was a doctor I had never met before. Friends come in many forms and ages, so don't feel that your friends can only come from your school or your grade.

YOUR POWER

Everyone deserves to be happy. Together we can make things better at schools and everywhere else. You shouldn't have to worry all day long about what a bully is going to say or do. They aren't worth a second of your time.

Bullies don't have the right or the true power to make you feel worthless, scared, or small. You matter. Love yourself and others will love you. As long as you are honest, caring, and respectful, you will lead others down the same road.

I've said before that bullies take away people's power. Bullies have a lot of ways to do this. They put bad thoughts in their victims' minds. The victims don't focus on how they feel about being bullied. Instead, they focus on the bad emotions. What happens is the bully is savvy enough to know that he is messing with your emotions. So, your negative emotions will be triggered, which are scary to you. Get a hold of your pure and positive emotions like anticipation and trust, both of which you need to let go of the negative emotions. This will make it easier to stand up to the bully and look him in the eyes and say, "I don't have the time or the need to deal with you."

You've just now used all of your good emotions versus your bad emotions. Don't misunderstand: bad emotions don't necessarily mean you can't use them. I'm just saying there is a time and a place to use them. And whenever it comes to a bullying issue, the circumstances need the right emotions to allow you to not fall under the "victim" category.

Fortunately, there are lots of ways to get your power back. When something goes wrong, understand that you need to change your reaction. Then you'll be able to take the steps to make it better. The best way is to not give your power away in the first place! Realize that you are who you are. People who pretend to be something they aren't don't have the power to defend themselves from bullies.

No one else can be you and you can't be anyone else. When you are confident in yourself, a bully can't control you. You already have the best way to stop anything negative from happening, and that's you!

8

Education

A friend of mine decided to travel across town to attend my school. Since there were plenty of good schools in her own area, her decision seemed a little strange. This friend soon turned into a bully. And because the class was very small, no one enjoyed her company.

She tried to physically and mentally bully me. When no one was looking, she would corner me and push her body against mine. She said things like I was jealous of her. After a couple of weeks, I scheduled a meeting with the teacher and the principal. I told them I was considering changing schools if nothing was done about her.

The next morning, she was moved to a different class. The teacher told me that the girl was going to be watched carefully to make sure she didn't bully anyone else. The parents were told about the school's actions. From then on whenever I had to be in the same place with her, I basically stayed away from her.

In my view, the main reason teachers don't get involved is because bullying usually doesn't happen when they're around. Teachers must start talking about bullying in class. The solution must involve everyone in school, including teachers and parents.

Now, you might come across parents who say that bullying is normal. They'll shrug and claim that kids just need to deal with it. Let me say right here that bullying is not normal. Parents must be willing to help! In cases where parents decide not to get involved, you can go to the school for support. If there is a teacher, principal, or counselor you trust, then there is someone who will step in.

"Bullying is not normal!"

EDUCATION STARTS AT HOME

Bullying is not normal in any way. Bullies have issues like feeling sad, low self-esteem, and difficulty with everyday life. How is that normal? Parents and other adults might think bullying is normal because it occurs constantly. They are just confusing the norm for normal. They are not the same. Instead of learning about the problem, they claim it's normal. As funny as it sounds, it's easier to say that than it is to take action.

Parents who think bullying is normal need to look at their own behaviors. They set the tone. If those parents would just open their eyes, they might recognize that their child is a bully. Parents need to teach their children how to treat others. When the parents of victims say that bullying is normal, their child is in a tough situation.

One of the things I would say to those parents is that it took a lot of courage for their child to talk about being bullied. When someone reaches out for help, it's likely that the bullying has been going on for a long time. Parents must support their child and the anti-bullying team. If physical bullying is involved, it must be reported to the authorities.

Anyone who hurts a child should be stopped. If the parents don't seem convinced, try meeting with a teacher, counselor, or principal. If the parent wants to help after hearing from the school administrators, then the adults can discuss the next step.

SUCCESS STORY: ADULT SOLUTIONS

A girl in my class named Melissa was really smart and sweet. She was bullied severely, mostly physically, by a boy in the same class. He must have shoved and pushed her well over fifty times. Every time it was brought up to the teachers, they claimed they never saw anything. On top of that, no one ever told Melissa's parents.

> "Every adult has to become part of the solution!"

I told my mom what I saw, and my mother was so worried about Melissa that she talked to the principal. When nothing changed, my mom joined me for lunch and asked Melissa for her parents' phone number. She was afraid to tell her parents about her bully. When my mother called Melissa's father, he left work and went straight to the school. He pulled her out of class and said that until the school made it safe for his daughter, she would not be back.

Sometimes it takes a lot of work to get help. Don't ever stop reaching out. If one person won't help, go to someone else!

AT-HOME BULLYING

In many cases bullying comes from home, where parents bully their own children. And usually that, in turn, creates bullies out of their own child. But, in Travis's case, the bullying he endured at home turned him into a victim for others to bully him.

Travis's mom, a military wife to his stepfather, occupied her time selling cosmetics and Tupperware. Travis brought his lunch in Tupperware, instead of brown bags like the other kids. Right away, the first week of junior high, the name "Tupperware Boy" caught on with kids. Travis was very quiet and shy; all he wanted to do was sit down and eat and maybe make friends. Instead he got yelled at by a girl to never sit next to her; she referred to him as "Tupperware Boy" and the rest of the school followed in her footsteps until his freshman year in high school.

At home, Travis's stepfather bullied Travis and his mother. Travis felt an overwhelming feeling of not being able to escape the constant pain. Neither home, nor school, nor church, where he was also bullied in a youth group, was safe. He was so angry that he began to feel himself turning into a monster. This is not the first time I've heard this.

In Travis's situation, he felt there was no one there to talk to. The adults in his life at the time were victims of bullying too. He controlled his anger though, and didn't let it define him. He worked through his past and created a future that he was in control of. He broke the cycle of bullying at home, and today is a strong, loving person. Learning from his own experience, Travis is a wonderful father and friend. He is now at the happiest stage in his life. It just goes to show, when something negative happens in your life, try your best to keep a positive mindset, know that your thoughts are yours to control, and that positive thoughts will lead to positive actions.

There is also a form of bullying that happens in the home that occurs between siblings. It doesn't matter who is younger or who is older, but there are so many siblings who take "fighting" to a new level. They harm each other emotionally by calling each other names or even hazing each other in their own home. Meghan was bullied by a sibling, and it turned out to affect her in deep ways.

Meghan was only eleven years old when her father died and her entire life went downhill. Her mother, an aspiring actress, juggled between work and rehearsals and was rarely home. Meghan was always a good student, but when she entered seventh grade, she had already changed schools twice due to bullying. By this time, Meghan felt hated by the world.

Even at home, Meghan's sister called her names, spit on her, and made her feel horrible about herself. She was also treated as the family servant, having hardly any time for herself. Her first suicide attempt was at the age of twelve. Her father has passed on, her mother was never home, and her sisters were dealing with struggles of their own—while also bullying her. Meghan believed she was alone and hopeless. She never thought to reach out to someone because bullying was never talked about in school or at home.

Sometimes a victim of bullying can rebel in a way to put up a wall between them and the hurt. Meghan didn't do this by becoming a bully herself, but she got involved in criminal activity and bad habits, including smoking. She was even sent to a school for "juvenile criminals." After being in and out of mental hospitals, Meghan was denied support from her mother after a cry for help. Meghan climbed out of her second story bedroom window and jumped, hoping to end the pain at the age of fifteen. She survived the jump with a broken sternum, ribs, and both legs. Meghan had no choice but to go through a healing process after this suicide attempt.

Meghan was lucky that something clicked inside her head. She came to understand that the solution to end her pain was not to kill herself, but to remove herself from the pain.

Meghan eventually managed to leave her hometown and move in with her aunt in Texas. Finding herself, spending lots of time hanging out at the library, she began making new friends. As days passed, her confidence grew. Her feeling of worthlessness became less and less.

Sitting at the library hearing her story, I asked Meghan, "If you could tell one child who is thinking about suicide something, what would it be?" Meghan replied, "The only thing that matters in this life is that you are happy with yourself. If you love someone, anyone—a little sister, brother, niece, nephew, or even a pet—just be with those you love." At the time of writing this book, Meghan was in love and engaged to be married. I am happy that I met her . . . alive.

TEACHING ADULTS

Teachers must know that students are willing to be part of the solution. Teachers can gain an understanding of victims' fears by sitting in on the anti-bullying team meetings. All teachers should be given the names of team members. Open and easy communication will ensure the anti-bullying program can work.

Once a teacher learns that bullying has happened, they should speak to the principal. They should also talk to the parents of the bully and the victim. Schools should also set up a parent-teacher agreement to support the anti-bullying teams.

Parents can be made aware of anti-bullying teams through a parent newsletter. It's important that the newsletter be endorsed by the principal. The teams can also be discussed during parent/teacher meetings. The idea is to let parents know that the teams are serious about getting rid of bullying and that no bullying, large or small, will be tolerated.

Questions parents should ask teachers, counselors, and the head person making the final decision include:

- What does my child need from me?

- What has my child tried to do to help?

- What is my child's main fear?

- Who is bullying my child?

Parents who sit in on anti-bullying team meetings

can also help to supervise areas at school where most incidents occur and become part of the solution. Both teachers and parents should recognize that their own behaviors have an impact on the amount of bullying that goes on. Teachers and parents should establish trust with their students and children. Everyone, including the adults, shares the same school!

PEACE AT SCHOOL

A school is a building where people gather to learn. The people in the building are the ones who must learn that it is their role to be peacemakers. That's why I mentioned earlier in my discussion on anti-bullying teams that every person in the school must act as a bystander, even if not part of the official anti-bullying team. Peace at school takes learning techniques as well as all students learning to resolve disagreements and coexist. It requires school administration overseeing and agreeing to a technique and experiment with what works and what doesn't. The way to do this is through communication. There is just no other way.

Demonstrations of ideas have to come in to play. If something doesn't work, don't spend too much time on it. Change it. And if something works, sticking to it is the key. And try to always remember that teachers are human and are learning how to deal with bullies as much as you are. So if there is something you can help them learn, communicate and share your views. Teachers and administrators are more than willing to listen.

WAYS ADMINISTRATORS CAN HELP

School announcements can help spread the word about the anti-bullying teams. Announcements can also show students how easy it is to get help. Some ideas for daily announcements are:

- ✤ Introduce the anti-bullying team members.
- ✤ Dates and times of meetings.
- ✤ Announce the Help Box location.
- ✤ Recruit new members.
- ✤ Encourage students to reach out to victims.

Anti-bullying teams can be a powerful force in your school. Since a bully's power is false, it can't stand up against the real power of a group. From your first meeting, you'll be on the way to making your school a bully-free zone!

A Final Word

Bullying affects kids and adults equally. I hope this book will leave something behind for you, no matter what age you are. I hope teachers find this book helpful because what you do every day is amazing and underrated, especially trying to do it with bullying complicating your days. I hope parents feel a bit more connected to what is happening in schools these days and how complex the dynamics between children have become. For all the kids, whether bullied, bullies, or bystanders, I hope you are encouraged to take power into your own hands and come together to end a needless practice and move forward for the well-being of yourself and others.

And for everyone else reading this book, I hope you turn to help a child in need, even if he or she is not yours. Everyone needs to do their part in order to have kids go to school to learn without fear, anxiety, or distraction. If this could happen, our next generation will become strong future leaders, because you never know, that leader just might be that *one kid* you helped that *one day*.

Dear Friend,

Always remember:

The key to reduce bullying is the bystander and you!

My space is my sanctuary, and bullies are not welcome!

If a cactus pokes you, it hurts, but you won't die. When you are bullied, it hurts, but the pain will only be lethal if you let it!

Dream big! Dreams can only come true if you're living in them.

Your age doesn't matter. If I can do it, so can you!

From me to you,

Shanaya

APPENDIX

Fast Facts

A new study out of the United Kingdom conducted by researcher Ian Rivers of Brunel University asked bullies why they bully.

Those with the most hostility reported picking on kids who were not good at sports. The most frequent bullying involved picking on kids who were perceived to be gay or lesbian. The research also indicates that beliefs or ideals of a specific community or society may influence bullying behavior. For example, if a school is sports-oriented, the kids who are not good at sports will be victimized by others for not living up to the expectation of others.

Source: http://www.livescience.com/11163-bullies-bullying.html

A study by Kathryn R. Wentzel and Carolyn C. Mc-Namara, both of University of Maryland, College Park, investigated the contribution of peer acceptance, perceived support from peers, and family cohesion to prosocial behavior in young adolescents. (Prosocial behavior occurs when someone acts to help another person, particularly when they have no goal other than to help a fellow human.) The study supported that being accepted by peers had a direct relation to prosocial behavior.

Source: http://jea.sagepub.com/content/21/1/29.short

The relationship between depression, anxiety, and bully/victim status is the basis of this study conducted in a Midwestern middle school. The groups included bullies, victims, bully-victims (bullies who are themselves bullied), and students without bully/victim problems (defined as "no status" for this study). Findings indicate that bully-victims and bullies were more likely to be depressed than victims and no status students. Bully-victims and victims were more likely to experience anxious symptoms than bullies or no status students. Thus, bully-victims may be the most impaired group with respect to depression and anxiety.

Source: http://psycnet.apa.org/psycinfo/2003-00452-006

Related research findings challenge the stereotypes of both high school bully and victim, indicating that the road to high school popularity can be dangerous. Various forms of teenage aggression and victimization occur throughout the social ranks as students jockey to improve their status. Those near the top of social hierarchy are often both perpetrators and victims of aggressive behavior, according to Robert Faris, author of the University of California, Davis study, "What we think often is going on is that this is part of the way kids strive for status. Rather than going after kids on the margins, they might be targeting kids who are rivals."

Source: http://well.blogs.nytimes.com/2011/02/14/web-of-popularity-weavedby-bullying/

Source: http://edition.cnn.com/2011/10/10/us/ac-360-bullying-study/index.html

A study comparing the proactive and reactive aggression in boys and girls aged ten to twelve years old found bully-victims to be the most aggressive group of all—both reactively (when provoked) and proactively (initiating the aggression).

Source: http://onlinelibrary.wiley.com/doi/10.1002/ab.90004/abstract

The results of a study assessing bullying and psychological disturbance among elementary school-aged children indicated that:

✤ More girls than boys were found to be involved in bullying.

✤ Bully-victims scored highest in externalizing behavior and hyperactivity, and they themselves reported feelings of ineffectiveness and interpersonal problems.

✤ Victims scored highest in internalizing behavior, psychosomatic symptoms, and reported anhedonia (the inability to gain pleasure from experiences that should be enjoyable).

✤ Children involved in bullying, especially those who were both bullies and bullied themselves, were psychologically disturbed.

✤ The probability of being referred for a psychiatric consultation was highest among bully-victims.

Source: http://www.sciencedirect.com/science/article/pii/ S0145213498000490

"Cyberbullying Identification, Prevention, and Response" by Sameer Hinduja, Ph.D., and Justin W. Patchin, Ph.D., of the Cyberbullying Research Center, cite two challenges today that make it difficult to prevent cyberbullying. First, many people don't see the harm associated with it and feel that there are more serious forms of aggression to worry about. We need to accept that cyberbullying is one problem that will only get more serious if ignored.

The other challenge involves a question: Who is willing to step up and take responsibility for responding to inappropriate use of technology? Parents often say that they don't have the technical skills to keep up with their kids' online behavior; teachers are afraid to intervene in behaviors that often occur away from school; and law enforcement is hesitant to get involved unless there is clear evidence of a crime or a significant threat to someone's physical safety. As a result, cyberbullying incidents often slip through the cracks; then the behavior can continue and escalate because it is not quickly addressed.

We need to collectively create an environment where kids feel comfortable talking with adults about this problem and feel confident that meaningful steps will be taken to resolve the situation. We also need to get everyone involved—youth, parents, educators, counselors, law enforcement, social-media companies, and the community at large. It will take a concerted and comprehensive effort from all stakeholders to make a difference in reducing cyberbullying.

Preventing Cyberbullying—
Top Ten Tips

1. Educate yourself—Research what it is as well as how and where it is likely to occur. Talk to your friends about what they are seeing and experiencing.

2. Protect your password—Never leave passwords or other identifying information where others can see it. Also, never give out this information to anyone, even your best friend.

3. Keep photos "PG"—Before you post that sexy image of yourself, consider if it's something you would like your parents, grandparents and the rest of the world to see. Bullies can use this picture as ammunition to make life miserable for you.

4. Never open unidentified or unsolicited messages—This includes emails, text messages, Facebook messages, etc. Delete them without reading. They could contain viruses. Also, never click on links to pages sent from someone you don't know—this may be a virus designed to collect your personal information.

5. Log out of online accounts—Don't save passwords in form fields within websites or your web browser for convenience, and don't stay logged in when you walk away from your computer or cell phone. Don't give anyone the slightest chance to pose as you online through your device. If you for-

get to log out of Facebook when using the computer at the library, the next person who uses that computer could get into your account and cause significant problems for you.

6. Pause before you post—Don't post anything that might compromise your reputation. People will judge you based on how you appear to them online. You could be given or denied jobs, scholarships, internships based on this.

7. Raise awareness—Start a movement, create a club, build a campaign, or host an event to bring awareness to cyber-bullying.

8. Set up privacy controls—Restrict access of your online pro-file to trusted friends only. Most social-networking sites offer you the ability to share certain information with friends only, but these settings must be configured to ensure maximum protection.

9. Google yourself—Regularly search your name in every major search engine (Google, Bing, Yahoo, etc.). If any per-sonal information or photo comes up what may be used by cyberbullies to target you, take action to have it removed before it becomes a problem.

10. Don't be a cyberbully yourself—Treat others how you would want to be treated. By being a jerk to others online, you are reinforcing the idea that the behavior is acceptable.

Source: http://www.cyberbullying.us/

BULLYING AND POSTTRAUMATIC STRESS

Dr. Stephen Joseph of the University of Warwick, United Kingdom, has researched bullying and posttraumatic stress and the impact of bullying on the self-worth of adolescent victims. His study suggests that one-third of bullied children suffer from clinically significant levels of posttraumatic stress. Rather than helping to toughen up students, as was once thought, bullying could seriously affect their mental health.

All types of bullying result in lower self-esteem, but social manipulation, such as excluding the victim from taking part in games, is more likely to lead to posttraumatic stress, and verbal taunts typically lead to lower self-worth. The study also suggests that these types of bullying lead to feelings of helplessness in the victim— that they lack control over their own feelings and actions. Those who feel that power and control lie within the bully instead of within the victim are much more likely to suffer from posttraumatic stress or lower self-worth.

Dr. Joseph states: "It is important that peer victimization is taken seriously, as symptoms such as insomnia, anxiety and depression are common among victims and have a negative impact on psychological health."

http://www.sciencedaily.com/releases/2003/04/030417080610.htm

THE SIX MYTHS OF BULLYING

Sandra Graham, a bullying special edition contributor at education.com, sites six myths of bullying:

MYTH #1 *Bullies are rejected by their peers and have no friends.*

Research shows that many bullies have high status in the classroom and lots of friends, particularly during middle school when they are perceived to be especially "cool."

MYTH #2 *Bullies have low self-esteem.*

There is not much research to support this, and many bullies perceive themselves in a positive light, sometimes displaying inflated self-views that can encourage them to rationalize their antisocial actions.

MYTH #3 *Being a victim builds character.*

Research finding clearly show that bullying experiences increase the vulnerabilities of children.

MYTH #4 *Many childhood victims of harassment become violent as teens.*

The truth is that most victims of bullying are more likely to suffer in silence than to retaliate.

MYTH #5   *There is a victim personality.*

Although certain personality characteristics, such as the tendency to be shy or withdrawn, place children at a higher risk for being bullied, there are situational factors (being a new student in school) or social factors (not having a friend) that increase the likelihood of a child being bullied. Situational factors explain why there are more temporary rather than chronic victims of bullying.

MYTH #6   *Bullying involves only perpetrators and victims.*

Bullying incidents are typically public (rather than private) events that have witnesses. Often, bullies are reinforced because those watching are passive and do nothing to help the victim.

In another well-documented report, Adrienne Nishina, also a Bullying Special Edition Contributor, states: "Negative social interactions are experienced as particularly stressful. Stress causes the body to secrete the stress hormone cortisol. Cortisol impairs immune system functioning, leaving the individual more vulnerable and less able to combat physical illnesses."

The following address some specifics:

Is There a Connection Between Bullying and Health?

✤ Children who are bullied are more likely to report experiencing migraine and non-migraine headaches than are their non-bullied counterparts.

✤ Students who get picked on frequently also miss more school because of both excused and unexcused absences.

Bullying Appears to Affect Students' Academic Performance.

✤ It isn't surprising that when students feel sick, depressed, worried, and/or isolated and alone, it is hard for them to perform to their potential in school. Feeling sick and thinking about or anticipating bullying may interfere with students' ability to concentrate, which can reduce their ability to learn new material. Students who felt down and sick as a function of bullying were absent from school more often and obtained lower grades.

✤ Interestingly, at least for physical symptoms, the reverse was not true. That is, whereas being bullied predicted later physical symptoms, kids who experienced a lot of physical symptoms did not later report getting bullied more. It may be that being sick limits bullying by peers and increases sympathy from others.

TAKE HOME MESSAGES

❖ Frequent physical complaints may be warning signs that a child is being bullied. School nurses and office staff, in addition to parents and teachers, are likely to encounter students who complain of physical symptoms. Especially when such complaints take place during certain classes or activities, adults may want to monitor the child inconspicuously to see if bullying is contributing to the problem. For example, students frequently try to avoid physical education (PE) classes by reporting physical complaints. In some cases, this may be the results of avoiding the physical activities. However, in other cases, this may be a response to being bullied.

❖ When youth report feeling sick, even if the symptoms appear to be socially motivated, they may not be "faking it." Such symptoms may be and feel real to the child. Additionally, legitimate frequent illnesses may have their roots in bullying. Social stress associated with bullying may lead children to become more vulnerable to illness.

✤ Teachers and other adults in children's lives at school can help by limiting students' exposure to bullying. Adult involvement includes discretely intervening in bullying incidents both inside and outside (e.g., during lunch, recess, passing period) of the classroom. Public intervention may also be warranted when the bullying is public and observed by other students. Teachers and school staff should consistently intervene whenever a bullying incident comes to their attention. The events that adults observe is a fraction of what students encounter on a daily basis. Not only can adult intervention serve to reduce the physical toll on youth, but it can alleviate the psychological impact as well.

Source: http://www.education.com/topic/school-bullying-teasing/

Acknowledgments

There are so many people that have touched my life that I would never have walked the path I'm walking without each and every single one of them. I'd like to take the opportunity to thank them now:

My mom has been with me through it all. Every single step of the way, every ten steps back and one step forward. She carries my spirit entirely in her heart. Without her, my life would not even be close to what it is today. She is my best friend and the captain of the ship that never sails too far away . . . Thank you, Mama.

My dad. I have never met anybody in my entire life who is as strong as my father. He is the one who catches everything that has fallen apart and puts it all back together better than it was before. If you ever read about superheroes, that's my dad; my mom always says to me, "You're a rock, just like your dad." One day I will repay you, Dad, for everything you have ever done for me, and more. I am proud to be your daughter.

Randy Peyser, my guardian angel, who fought leaps and bounds for the best fit possible for my book and me. There is nothing I can't ever go to her for. She is like the groundskeeper for the growth of my book-writing career and much more. I am honored to call you my beautiful friend.

Thank you, Kathleen Ronald, my speaking catalyst, and my family: Grandma and Grandpa, Uncle Gil and Trisha, Alex and Myrna, my cousins Adrian and Jessica, my dear friend and little helper, Silvia Chamlee, and my Grandpa in Germany. And thank you to all my friends— old and new. I love spending time and hanging out with you.

Lifetime gratitude to each and every single one of my readers. I will never forget how each one of you believed in me and never doubted me for even a second in my career and in the choices I made and continue to make. My amazing world is only amazing because you all are in it.

Index

About the Author

Shanaya Fastje launched her career as a published author at the age of eight and became an inspirational speaker at the age of ten when she entered the first of her popular Mystery School series in a national book-writing contest and was selected "extraordinary book" from over 3,000 entrants. Two more volumes followed before she turned her attention to developing a hugely successful presidential award-winning anti-bullying program, which has been outlined in this book.

Shanaya has been called upon to speak before tens of thousands of people, spreading the message that "bullies are all about power, this power is fake, and the real power is with the bystander and the victims." Applying her deep understanding of the dynamics of bullying, she successfully averted several tragic child suicides through individual coaching.

Shanaya is the recipient of many awards, including one by President Barack Obama, Governor Rick Perry, and by her hometown of El Paso, Texas, which also proclaimed March 15, 2011, Shanaya Fastje Day.

Homeschooled at her request since she was nine years old, Shanaya is now thirteen and has graduated high school. A talented musician, composer, and actress, she is currently writing her fifth book—her first fiction novel—in hopes for the possibility of adaption for film or television. She has recorded her first single and music video with aspirations for an album.

Shanaya now lives in Los Angeles, California, where she is further developing all areas of her career. Visit Shanaya at www.shanayafastje.com and on Facebook. "Like" her fan pages "The Bully in the Mirror" and "Shanaya Fastje Author" or follow Shanaya on Twitter @ShanayaFastje.